JUDSON PRESS

PUBLISHERS SINCE 1824

D0822543

Got STYLE?
PERSONALITY-BASED
EVANGELISM

Turning
Traditional
Evangelism
on Its Head

got style?

personality-based evangelism

JEFFREY A. JOHNSON

Edited by
Patricia G.
Duckworth

Foreword by
David C. Laubach

JUDSON PRESS
PUBLISHERS SINCE 1824
VALLEY FORGE, PA

got style? personality-based evangelism

Names have been changed in the anecdotes and illustrations to protect the privacy of the individuals.

Judson Press has made every effort to trace the ownership of all quotes. In the event of a question arising from the use of a quote, we regret any error made and will be pleased to make the necessary correction in future printings and editions of this book.

Unless otherwise indicated, all Scriptures are taken from the *Holy Bible, New International Version®. NIV®.* Copyright ©1973, 1978, 1984 by International Bible Society. Used by permission of Zondervan. All rights reserved.

Scriptures marked TNIV are taken from the Holy Bible, Today's New International Version™. Copyright ©2001, 2005 by the International Bible Society®. All rights reserved worldwide.

Library of Congress Cataloging-in-Publication Data
Johnson, Jeffrey A.
Got style?: personality-based evangelism/Jeffrey A. Johnson; Patricia G. Duckworth, editor.—1st ed. p. cm. Includes bibliographical references.
ISBN 978-0-8170-1555-8 (pbk.: alk. paper) 1. Evangelistic work—Psychology. 2. Personality—Religious aspects—Christianity. I. Duckworth, Patricia G. II. Title.
BV3793.J612 2009
269'.2—dc22   2009017897

I dedicate this book to Rev. William R. Hoffman, who went home to be with the Lord in 2002 at the much-too-early age of fifty-eight. Not only was he my mentor in ministry, but he was really the only dad I ever knew. He taught me more about ministry through example than a library of books or a seminary of classes. His impact and importance are still very much a part of who I am and what I do. I miss him to this day.

Just a week before he died, he shared with me that, metaphorically speaking, he was at the top of his game in his personal and pastoral life. The irony of that statement was played out at his unexpected passing. He departed this world while playing basketball (a game he loved) at his local YMCA, leaving that court for the courts of heaven, a place he loved to preach about. Who could ask for anything more?

And just for the record, he made the three-point shot before he headed home.

I also wish to dedicate this book to the loves of my life:
my Lord Jesus,
my wife, Karen,
and our two children, Jonae Allayna and Judson Adoniram.
They all make my life worth living!

contents

foreword

When Christians learn that only 10 percent of believers have the spiritual gift of evangelism, many breathe a huge sigh of relief. They are "off the hook," to use a fishing metaphor. I don't think so! We are all in the fishing business (see Mark 1:17). Like the Twelve we are called to be witnesses in Jerusalem, Judea, Samaria, and the uttermost part of the earth (Acts 1:8). All of the spiritual gifts—from administration to compassion, from giving to teaching—can be used in the service of that Great Commission.

Beyond our Spirit-given qualities, we each hold another unique gift—our life experience. Far more effective than rote-memorized Bible verses and scripted responses to seekers' questions is our individual story about our life of faith and experience with God. Such a story is a testimony that cannot be refuted.

Moreover, long before any of us discovered our spiritual gifts or experienced much of life at all, we received another gift from God: our personality. Those who study personality types believe that these personality preferences are hard-wired at birth, and the psalmist wrote that it was God who knit us together in our mother's womb (Psalm 139:13). It is our God-given personality that largely determines how we communicate with and relate to one another in community. The good news is that people of all personality types can be effective evangelists, each in his or her own distinctive style. This is the heart of Jeffrey Johnson's *Got Style? Personality-based Evangelism.*

God weaves together the Spirit's gifts, our life experiences, and our innate personality to prepare us uniquely and individually to share the Good News with our neighbors and with the next generation of disciples. Our "style" of communicating will be different from believer to believer but, according to Johnson, all can be powerfully and profoundly transforming in the lives of our family members, friends, neighbors, and coworkers. Whether we operate primarily in a words-based style of the assertive, analytic, or storytelling personality or through the works-based style of the relational, invitational, or incarnational personality, we are uniquely qualified and equipped by God to communicate the gospel in relationship with our world.

Our Trinitarian theology teaches us that the very nature of God is the relationship between Father, Son, and Holy Spirit. When Jesus envisioned the church he linked relationship to evangelism (John 17:21). It was relationships that defined the early church in Acts. It was difficulty with relationships that caused problems for Paul's churches. No wonder, then, that our natural style of communicating, of forming relationships, prepares us for a faith-sharing encounter with someone who does not yet have a relationship with God.

Yes, there are those with an extraordinary gift for communicating the gospel across cultures, languages, interests, and personalities. But we who are average fisherfolk may have confidence in the gifts we possess—that the Lord will provide opportunities for us to share our own stories in our own ways. And where the connection seems broken or garbled, we may trust the Holy Spirit to do the work of translation—just as effectively as the people experienced at Pentecost. "How beautiful are the feet of those who bring good news!" (Isaiah 52:7) is not just encouragement for professional clergy, vocational evangelists, and missionaries, but for all us who communicate "what comes naturally" and discover that we've Got Style.

—David C. Laubach, MDiv, DMin
Associate Executive Director
Strategic Missional Relations
National Ministries, American Baptist Churches USA

preface

Jeff Johnson's book, *Got Style? Personality-based Evangelism*, is a perfect fit for my West Coast culture, which a Lutheran scholar termed "The None Zone." It is a culture where polite society prefers none of the traditional religious options. It is a zone where Jesus might be good news, but the church of Jesus connotes bad news for so many. In this practical and conversational resource, Johnson blends the high touch for this high-tech culture by letting our personal witness emerge from our own individually unique wiring. It is an approach that is exactly right for this postmodern generation and a None Zone context.

Johnson's blend of strong biblical studies with contemporary illustrations, together with an amazing array of practical tools and recommended resource, combine to make *Got Style?* the book on evangelism that I will recommend in my church and for my school.

—Ray Bakke
Chancellor and professor
Bakke Graduate University
Former pastor and professor of evangelism and mission
Northern and Eastern Baptist Theological Seminaries
Senior Associate for Large Cities
The Lausanne Committee for
World Evangelization (1980–2000)

introduction for leaders

This book contains precepts and principles that I have learned and lived during nearly twenty years of local-church ministry as both a solo and a senior pastor. However, if you had gone looking for these concepts back in my earliest years in ministry, you might have had a hard time finding them in any coherent form. I was never able to formalize them as I share them with you now, not until 2001 when I became director of evangelism for the American Baptist Churches USA (ABCUSA) under the auspices of our Board of National Ministries, the arm of ABCUSA that works in the United States and Puerto Rico. I was afforded the precious gift of time to systemize my concepts and to read a great deal more on the subject of personality-based evangelism in particular and on ministry in general. I believe that what I share in this book has application across the spectrum of folks in your church as well as across the spectrum of ministry in your congregation.

Let me say from the outset, I am not the originator of many of the concepts of personality-based evangelism. I am really not sure who is. As I've been reminded by Scripture (Ecclesiastes 1:9) and by my colleague David Laubach, nothing is entirely new. Everything is recycled by rewording. This book is an offering of new perspectives and a linking of old ideas in new ways to meet the new challenges that face us.

Hippocrates, originator of the great oath taken by physicians, introduced basic personality concepts some three hundred years before Christ, but those concepts were not intended to be linked with evangelism. Some two hundred years after Christ, another doctor, Galen, created a detailed list of strengths and weaknesses based on

Hippocrates' concepts. Like Hippocrates, Galen did not observe these traits in terms of religion. Therefore, what I do here is more the work of a refiner. These general ideas have been "out there" in some form for centuries and more.

One of our American Baptist regional executive ministers told me he had taught some of this in the 1970s and early 80s in one of our ABC-related schools (when I was still a kid). Jard DeVille, who early on contributed to the area of evangelism based on personality, began in 1980 to advocate for an understanding of the link between personality and evangelism, using an elementary form with just four styles. Further, Duncan McIntosh said, "Evangelism has been used to describe quite a range of activities and styles of communicating the Good News."[1] More recently, these concepts became familiar to many when several groups, including the Evangelical Covenant denomination led by Lon Allison and the Willowcreek Church and Association led by Mark Mittelberg, formulated their ideas and put them into print. Others continue to probe and shape these ideas, and I will add my insights and experiences here.

This book is an attempt to bring together and refine the various evangelistic programs, methods, and curriculums into an understandable and applicable format, by categorizing them in order to complement specific personality styles. In the end, however, we all are seeking a renewed vision of God's heart, for while we are always trying to find better methods to share our faith, God is looking for better people.[2]

The premier book on the subject in recent history is *Tell It with Style: Evangelism for Every Personality Type* by Helen Boursier (Downers Grove, IL: InterVarsity Press, 1995). She based her work on the four basic personality styles included here and provided insights into the personalities from the perspectives of both the giver and receiver of communication. Though Helen's book is out of print, it is well worth reading. What follows is, in part, a tribute to her work, but I will provide a newer look at the subject and offer greater diversity and definition.

We live in a time where changes occur exponentially every year in every area of lives. For example,

1. Every two or three years, the knowledge base doubles.

2. Every day, seven thousand scientific and technical articles are published.

3. Satellites orbiting the globe send enough data to fill nineteen million volumes in the Library of Congress—every two weeks.

4. Today's high school graduates have been exposed to more information than their grandparents were in their entire lifetimes.

5. There will be as much change in the next three decades as there was in the last three centuries.[3]

The ways in which we engage with the world as messengers of the Good News must take into account our rapidly changing world, and it is clear that in our times, evangelism cannot occur in a vacuum or as something external to ourselves. The assessment of personality-based styles among a congregation's membership is actually just one component of aligning or realigning the congregation toward mission and outreach through styles-based evangelism, although it is the crucial and critical component. As tempting as it might be to jump right into the styles, we must keep in mind that styles are a part of a broader framework, the component steps of which are summarized below. Evangelism should occur naturally and normally as a part of health and spiritual vitality, individually and congregationally.

Seven Steps of Personality-Based Styles Outreach and Implementation

1. Discernment and Discovery among leadership
2. Vision casting
3. Prayer and hospitality training among congregation

4. Personality styles—evaluation, education, and explanation
5. Personality styles—styles specific training
6. Personality styles—styles organic training
7. Follow-up and discipleship

This book focuses primarily on step four with some input for training in step five. For a fuller explanation of these steps, see Appendix 1.

Personality-based evangelism affirms the diversity of God's creativity as seen in the Body of Christ. There is a place for everyone at the evangelistic table, where people can share their faith in ways that complement and do not compete with their inherent, divine wiring. Personality-based evangelism also acknowledges the diversity of the population outside the church and so presents the gospel in style-specific ways—literally speaking, the languages of their personalities. This book is an effort to address both of these realities.

NOTES
1. Duncan McIntosh, *The Everyday Evangelist,* Laura Alden, ed. (Valley Forge, PA: Judson Press, 1984), 8.
2. William Carr Peel and Walter Larimore, MD, *Going Public with Your Faith* (Grand Rapids: Zondervan, 2004), 196.
3. *Leadership and Technology,* National School Boards Association's Institute for the Transfer of Technology to Education, http://www.nsba.org/sbot/toolkit/chnsoc.html.

CHAPTER 1

the premise

Note to the Reader and Leader: As you begin to investigate all that this subject of personality-based evangelism has to offer, I strongly urge you *first* take the personal assessment in Chapter 8. If you complete this *first*, the contents of this book will be much more helpful and rewarding.

Before we examine the premise of personality-based evangelism styles, let's briefly look at the relationships among evangelism, witnessing, and spiritual gifts. These ideas offer a firm footing for understanding the styles of evangelism.

True or false: You need to know your spiritual gifts to do evangelism effectively. Answer: False! That false perception is often preached by clergy and perpetuated by laity. For more than eighteen years, I have served as a pastor in the local-church setting. Throughout that time, and even in years prior, I have always had a problem with the assumption that people need to know their spiritual gifts in order for God to use them effectively in evangelism. It seemed to me that the early church did effective evangelism for decades, actually seeing larger-scale conversions than we have witnessed today, without the benefits of the lists of or training about spiritual gifts. It was centuries later that lists were widely disseminated for comparison purposes.

This false premise of the relationship of evangelism and gifts needs to be replaced with a better understanding of witnessing. Surprising as it might sound, the term *witnessing* is not a scriptural term. *Being a witness*, on the other hand, is entirely scriptural. Being a witness is not merely something you do. Being a witness to Jesus is something you are, if you are Jesus' followers. *Witnessing* is a verb, a mechanical process. *Being a witness* is a noun, an organic reality.[1] The moment you become a Christian, you become a unique witness of Christ, as unique as God made you. What qualifies you to be a witness for Christ is spending time with Christ. Therefore, every believer, every Christ-follower is a witness. Jesus said it best, "You shall *be* my witnesses" (Acts 1:8, emphasis added). A witness is who you are, not what you do.

Pastor and blogger Heather Kirk-Davidoff has observed that for many, the term *witness* suggests, first and foremost, someone who speaks about his or her experience or expertise in the context of a court proceeding. When she asked her lawyer-filled church in Washington, DC, what was required of someone to be a good witness, she received this response: "A good witness tells the truth and has the perceived credibility to back it up."[2]

How then does a witness establish credibility? In addition to all sorts of little factors like having polished shoes, her lawyers listed these factors:

1. Good witnesses look the decision maker (judge or jury) in the eyes when answering a question. They do not look down or look around the room.

2. Good witnesses speak in a confident manner—they don't hesitate or stumble over their words. They are not intimidated when cross-examined.

3. Good witnesses listen carefully to the questions they are asked. If they don't understand a question, they ask for clarification before responding.

4. Good witnesses answer the questions they are asked directly and stop talking when they've given their answers.

5. Good witnesses speak in plain language that every listener can understand.

6. Good witnesses do not argue when questioned.

But of all these factors, everyone agreed that the most important one was this:

7. If they do not know the answer to a question, good witnesses say so. They don't try to make something up. They do not speculate.[3]

At this point, you may be aware of an assumption I make about evangelism in general: I believe there is some point in time when a person makes a conscious decision to follow Christ. This can happen in any Christian tradition or outside all Christian influences. The decision may happen suddenly, as in the apostle Paul's case, or it may happen gradually, as in Timothy's case, where he grew up with a believing mother and grandmother (2 Timothy 1:5). However it happens, becoming a disciple of Jesus is something people choose and accept, rather than something that "just happens" to them from the outside. I believe that people come into God's family by their own choices, not by the words or choices of others. Since that is the case, people need an opportunity to make that decision. Our evangelistic efforts give them that opportunity.

A Place for Spiritual Gifts

So, if being a witness is about who we are in Christ, then what can we say about spiritual gifts? Where do they fit in?

In Paul's letters to the New Testament church, you will find descriptions of "spiritual gifts," including teaching, prophecy, healing, giving, apostleship, and in Ephesians 4:11, evangelism. (For other descriptive lists, see Romans 12:6-8; 1 Corinthians 12:1-14, 27-30.) All of these gifts are for the building up of the existing Body of Christ (i.e., discipleship). With the exception of the gift of evangelism, which we will look at in Chapter 2, the purpose of the gifts is not to add new members to the church through faith in Jesus (evangelism). Granted, people's understanding and use of spiritual gifts can enhance their ability to be witnesses, but their knowledge of their gifts is not a requirement to be a witness. In Scripture, witnessing is never linked with spiritual giftedness; evangelism and witness are always linked.

A second point needs to be made about the purpose of spiritual gifts. As I have said, spiritual giftedness is presented in Scripture for use in building up the Body of Christ. But we are not given our gifts in their fully matured form when we become followers of Jesus. Our understanding of such gifts and their usage comes to fruition as we grow in grace and gain an understanding of what God has given each of us to do. And this maturing process takes time. The Scriptures spell out clearly that people new to the faith should not be placed in roles or given responsibilities that may put undue pressure on them. That person "must not be a recent convert, or he may become conceited and fall" (1 Timothy 3:6). Because spiritual giftedness is that which is discovered as we mature in our Christian faith through a journey of discipleship, new believers should not be leaders in the congregation too early, lest they become overwhelmed by pressure and problems and falter in their walk with the Lord and other believers. The best discipleship is the "learn by doing" method, *but* the biblical model of learning places a more experienced and mature person as guide and mentor for a less-experienced Christian (e.g., Paul and Silas or Barnabas and Mark).

The third and most important aspect of spiritual gifts has to do with how quickly a new believer is meant to evangelize. Sharing our faith has less to do with the corporate church and more to do with the individual believer. However, the church needs to facilitate what comes naturally for individuals as they share their newfound faith.

When people come to faith in Jesus Christ, their biblical literacy and knowledge vary widely. While the mature use of gifts and growing up in Christ do include acquiring some knowledge of the Bible, expecting people to wait to share their faith until they have a general, adequate understanding of Scripture is problematic in two ways. First, who gets to decide what is adequate? Second, learning Scripture basics take time. And if people have little or no knowledge of the Bible when they come to faith in Christ, they might wait months or years to build that foundation. In the meantime, the energy and enthusiasm inherent in their conversion becomes stifled; passion wanes. New believers often become only hearers of the Word and not doers (James 1:22). New believers generally have twelve people in their spheres of influence who are not yet believers, while long-term Christians have about four on the average.[4] Taking new believers out of their spheres of influence for any length of time substantially limits the reach of the kingdom.

From a biblical point of view, however, there is no time limit when it comes to sharing the gospel. From the moment people experience salvation, they become witnesses, expected to share their faith experience, to introduce others to Christ. The Scripture's witness in John 1:40-42 records that within hours, Andrew shares his encounter with Christ with his brother, Peter. The next day, Philip—within hours of meeting Jesus—introduces his friend Nathanael to Christ. Studies show the closer one's conversion to Christ is to one's first conversation about Christ, the more often one will share one's faith over the course of time. The greater the lapse of time between eternal conversion and eventual conversation about it, the less likely people are to evangelize and evangelize regularly, if ever. One study states only 11 percent of church members shared the gospel even once in the last year and 33 percent have *never* shared the gospel with anyone.[5] What would account for this? Perhaps if we are honest, we will admit that the more leadership roles people take on in the church in order to "use their spiritual gifts," the less time they have for connections with people who are not yet believers.

Personality and Evangelism

The stories of Andrew and Phillip—and the experiences of other people I have known—have always led me to wonder exactly what it is that allows or enables people to share their faith with others so freely and so immediately after their conversions. It seems clear that a believer's early communication, then and now, is about a personal encounter and experience with Christ, not really about a doctrine or dogma. Why? The Holy Spirit certainly leads and moves people, and the Spirit's role cannot and will not be minimized. But is there also some God-given something in people with whom the Holy Spirit works that enables them to be early and effective witnesses, even without special training? I believe there is. My study and experience have led me to this conclusion:

> More than anything else, *personality* is the human component involved in effective evangelism.

By personality, I mean much more than the traditional dichotomy of extrovert vs. introvert, which pits three-fourths of the population against the other fourth, respectively. Extroverts and introverts can be found in varying degrees in any of the personality styles. Instead, by personality I mean God's inherent wiring as to how people engage and interact with the world.

People seem to instinctively know this, even if they have different ways of expressing it. A recent informal poll found only 8 to 10 percent of Christians regularly share Christ with others. When asked, "Why don't Christians share Christ?" several responses were given:

- 33.5 percent are afraid of being rejected, embarrassed.
- 21.7 percent are afraid of not having answers.
- 19.2 percent rarely think about the need.
- 17.3 percent don't know what to say.
- 8.3 percent haven't found a way to share that fits a personal style. (In other words, it's not comfortable or natural.)[6]

Although only the last response names personality specifically, personality seems to be behind the other responses as well; people are really saying that they haven't found a way to do evangelism naturally—as a part of how they are wired. Because evangelism has become associated with something unnatural or forced, it feels uncomfortable and threatening. I never understood why sharing something so good makes so many feel so bad, until I realized most people are doing evangelism in a way contrary to the way God made them. We are called to do evangelism out of "grace, not guilt. It can be enjoyable, not just an endurable experience."[7]

Having a very high view both of Scripture and of Jesus Christ as the Son of God, I believe an unbalanced perspective on either one leads us to dysfunctional ways of sharing our faith. A core of my belief system is that the Bible is the sole source for what I believe (faith) and should direct what I do (practice). Not having any formalized conceptions, I began openly and honestly searching the inspired pages for how Scripture views and values evangelism. While contemporary examples are helpful, they cannot replace New Testament examples. What I began to see was evidence that we all have this personality "thing," and it informs how we share Christ with others. One of the most striking examples of Spirit-used personality is in the book of Acts, where we read about Saul, whom we come to know later by his Greek name, Paul. Examining some of Paul's story will give us a glimpse of how the Spirit works with personality.

Paul was, from Scripture's earliest references, a passionate persecutor of those who held the new Christian faith. He was present at the martyrdom of Stephen and, though only watching over the outer garments (coats) of those who stoned Stephen, he was guilty by association.

> At this they covered their ears and, yelling at the top of their voices, they all rushed at him [Stephen], dragged him out of the city and began to stone him. Meanwhile, the witnesses laid their clothes at the feet of a young man named Saul (Acts 7:57-58).

Paul's passion finds further expression as he travels north to Damascus to, in his words, persecute the church of God (1 Corinthians 15:9) and to try to destroy it (Galatians 1:13). It is clear that, for Paul, this was more than completing a job task. He took his responsibility personally. Personality is very personal. For each of us, it is unique. It defines who we are and directs how we interact with others.

And yet it was en route to Damascus to carry out this persecution that Paul had a life-transforming encounter with Jesus Christ.

> Meanwhile, Saul was still breathing out murderous threats against the Lord's disciples. He went to the high priest and asked him for letters to the synagogues in Damascus, so that if he found any there who belonged to the Way, whether men or women, he might take them as prisoners to Jerusalem. As he neared Damascus on his journey, suddenly a light from heaven flashed around him. He fell to the ground and heard a voice say to him, "Saul, Saul, why do you persecute me?"
>
> "Who are you, Lord?" Saul asked.
>
> "I am Jesus, whom you are persecuting," he replied. "Now get up and go into the city, and you will be told what you must do" (Acts 9:1-6).

The record goes on to tell us that after only three days, Paul walked south on the same road, but he was changed from Christianity's greatest persecutor into Christianity's greatest promoter!

> Saul spent several days with the disciples in Damascus. At once he began to preach in the synagogues that Jesus is the Son of God. All those who heard him were astonished and asked, "Isn't he the man who raised havoc in Jerusalem among those who call on this name? And hasn't he come here to take them as prisoners to the chief priests?" Yet Saul

grew more and more powerful and baffled the Jews living in Damascus by proving that Jesus is the Christ (Acts 9:19-22).

What strikes me about Paul's story is this: It was only *three days* between the time he was an enemy of Christ and when he became a first-class friend of Christ. More striking is that he attended no online training program, no school of evangelism, no workshop or seminar. What did God's Spirit tap in Paul to move him to promote that which he passionately and intensely had persecuted days before? God used Paul's inherent assertive personality. Surrendering his entire life to the Spirit, *personality included,* was a part of Paul's transformation. With the same vigor, the same *personality,* Paul promoted the very thing he had tried to destroy.

Paul's conversion was evidence of the Spirit's working in his heart. Paul shared the gospel using his personality as he surrendered himself to the Holy Spirit. This was just one example in Scripture. I wondered if there were other kinds of evidence for how the Spirit views or uses personalities, so I searched Scriptures further. This is what I found: "If you *speak,* you should do so as one who speaks the very *words* of God. If you *serve,* you should do so with the *strength* God provides, so that in all things God may be praised through Jesus Christ" (1 Peter 4:11, TNIV, italics added). This verse indicates that everyone in the world fits into two broad groups: those who naturally engage the world by what they *say* and those who naturally engage the world by what they *do.* The first group uses words (verbal or written) and emphasizes the head. The second group uses works and emphasizes the hands. These two groups describe how we all are generally wired and how God has created us. However, when used by the Spirit, both of these personality types work together so God is revealed or acknowledged. In Paul's case (as in everyone's case), God just used the personality he had. Though Paul was clearly transformed from hating to loving Jesus, he did not become some other person.

Understanding people in light of 1 Peter 4, then, can be seen in a visual way if we put the evangelism styles on a chart (see Table 1). The styles on the left of the chart are proclamation styles: These individuals show their concern and share the gospel most naturally through what they *say*. The styles on the right are presence styles: These individuals show their concern and share the gospel most naturally through what they *do*. Looking further in Scripture,

PRIMARY STYLE	ASSERTIVE	ASSERTIVE	
Characteristics	Direct, Verbal	Direct, Verbal	
Occupations	Salesman	Salesman	
Substyle	a. Public	a. Personal	c. Phenomena 1. Prophetic 2. Power
Biblical Example	Peter	Philip the Deacon	Ananias
Scriptural Support	Acts 2:14-41	Acts 8:26-39	Acts 9:10-19
Modern Examples	Billy Graham Ann Graham-Lotz Luis Palau John Guest	Bill Bright Bill Fay D. James Kennedy Ray Comfort	Peter Wagner Jack Deere Charles Kraft Bill Johnson
Examples from the Life of Christ	People of Capernaum John 12	Nicodemus John 3	Woman with issue of blood Luke 8
	Preached, Repent Matthew 4:17	Preached Born Again John 3:3	W authority Mark 1:22
	WORDS		
	The Head "What We Say"		
	1 Peter 4:11 "whoever speaks..."		

Table 1

1 Peter 3:1 gives additional insight into the styles of presence, advising "if any of them do not believe the word, they may be won over without words by the behavior." Here, it is not what is said but what is done that can win people over. People who are basically *doing* people get their hearts and hands dirty in their evangelistic efforts. But just so there is no misunderstanding: Words also have a vital place. First Peter 3:15 reminds us that we should "always be

ANALYTICAL	STORYTELLING	RELATIONAL	INVITATIONAL	INCARNATIONAL
Logical, Rational	Engaging	People-oriented	Event-oriented	Needs-oriented
Engineer/Professor	Musician/Actor	Counselor/Teacher	Host/Planner 1. Home 2. Church	Nurse 1. Service 2. Servant
Paul	Woman at the Well	Philip the Disciple	Andrew	Dorcas
Acts 17:16-33	John 4:1-42	John 1:43-51	John 1:35-42 John 6:1-15 John 12:20-22	Acts 9:36-43
C.S. Lewis Lee Strobel Ravi Zacharias Josh McDowell	Dave Dravecky Joni Eareckson-Tada Corrie Ten Boom Tony Campolo	Becky Pippert Joe Aldrich Nicky Gumbel Bill Hybels	Crusade Attendees	Millard Fuller Franklin Graham Steve Sjogren Jimmy Carter
Rich Young Ruler Luke 18	—Parables Luke 15	Of Lost Things Zacchaeus Luke 19	Andrew John 1	Man at the Pool of Bethesda John 5
Asked Question (?) Taught the Way Matthew 22:16	Gave Analogies Spoke in parables Matthew 13:34	Was Friend of Sinners Luke 7:34	Invited Himself Luke 19:5	Came to Serve Matthew 20:26-28
		WORKS		
		The Hand "What We Do"		
		1 Peter 4:11 "whoever serves…"		

prepared to give an answer to everyone who asks [us] to give a reason for the hope that [we] have." This verse assumes our lives will cause people to want to know why—and we need to be ready with words to explain, because they will initiate the conversation and ask the questions.

It must also be understood here that evangelism is not about convicting, convincing, or converting the non-Christian. That is the work of God through the activity of the Holy Spirit in a person's heart. Evangelism is about persuasive presentation, using both speech (lips) and actions (life) to share the Good News. Presentation only appeals to a need already present in a person or that can be perceived during the encounter. Thus, evangelism is really about conversing with the person in such a way that communicates the gospel. Again, words and works are the two basic ways we can evangelize. God wired us with one or the other of these broad-based personality styles.

Though I have been touting this dichotomy for years, the most concise descriptors I've read about the contrast between words and works are presented in *Irresistible Evangelism: Natural Ways to Open Others to Jesus* by Sjogren, et al. Below are several pairings, representing two extremes of a continuum; word or proclamation styles are on the left, and works or presence styles are on the right.

Monologue	Dialogue
Presentations	Conversations
Our language	Their language
Quantity of *conversions*	Quality of *conversations*
Front door approaches	Back door approaches
Fishing from the bank	Swimming with the fish
Scripted	Spontaneous
Winning	Nudging
Gospel presentations	Gospel experiences[8]

I share these pairings because personality-based evangelism styles are like branches coming out of the trunk, which 1 Peter 4:11 describes as the reality of how God has made us.

Along the way, I did additional and concentrated reading and research.[9] I discovered that some people working in this field advocate as few as two or four personality types, splitting along the lines of extrovert vs. introvert. There are others who advocate as many as sixteen or twenty types, based in part on various configurations of the Myers-Briggs instrument. I feel that two or four styles are too restrictive, because people end up being pigeonholed. I believe twelve, sixteen, or twenty types are too many in relation to the context of evangelism because people have difficulty seeing and engaging their own primary and secondary styles. Their styles of strength become lost in the details of the concept.

After study and experience, I have found that six styles with several substyles provide the best useable framework. Others have done the same, though probably not for the same reasons.[10] I also wish to provide a substantial explanation of the styles and a co-opted and adapted evaluation instrument, so you might assess your own placement within the spectrum. Most importantly, I wish to offer some biblical examples for each style, which are generally missing in the other works. The goal is to give you a framework for evangelism that moderates the extremes of "an unannounced assault on a stranger [far left of Table 1] or little more than being nice to someone else [far right of Table 1]."[11]

As we move forward in this discussion, let me say emphatically: No one style is better than any other. No one personality is the perfect personality. They are all created by God and most useful when submitted to the lordship of Jesus and the leading of the Holy Spirit. Author Randy Becton adds, "Each person's unique personality and evangelistic style imprints the lives of those around him or her."[12] Of course, there are positives and negatives about each of the styles. "All personalities have strengths, that when pushed to excess become weaknesses."[13] So Joe Aldrich concludes, "We must recognize and affirm the legitimacy of [personality] styles and learn to live with the tensions they create."[14] You cannot change who you are, but you can temper your temperament.[15] In other words, you can and should mature in Christ, but you should not try to be someone you are not.

Additionally, 1 Peter 4 indicates that people are created to complement each other: "Successful mixing and matching of our own personality style with others takes a combination of common sense and practice."[16] I would add that it also takes the ever-present work of the Holy Spirit.

Before we begin our detailed discussion about the individual personality styles and their connections with evangelism, here are some important overall observations about the styles chart (Table 1) and the styles laid out therein. Moving from left to right, there are the following continuums.

Encounters IN time and encounters OVER time:
On the far left, the encounter between the person doing the evangelism and the person being evangelized can be calculated literally in minutes. It is brief and to the point. On the far right, the encounter or, more accurately, multiple encounters, last longer and longer, going from minutes to days to weeks to months and potentially even to years. The encounters on the left often occur just once. The encounters between people on the right are often many, providing people time in between to think about what has been shared. Out of a broad-based sample of people who have made a public profession of faith in the previous twelve months, 69 percent described their coming to faith as gradual, with the average time span being four years.[17]

Strangers and friends:
On the far left, the individuals involved, i.e., the evangelizer and the evangelized, are pretty much strangers. On the far right, they know

each other, sometimes intimately so, because of multiple contacts. For sure, on the right, the evangelizer and the evangelized are definitely acquaintances; it is probably safe to say that they are or are becoming friends. On the left hand side, there has not been much, if any, building of relationship—it might not even be a high value of the evangelizer. Because the encounter is brief on the far left, the evangelizer quickly gets to the point since there is no previous, cherished relationship to lose. On the right, time is taken because of the value placed on the already-present relationship.

Talking and listening:
On the far left of the chart, the evangelizer does most of the talking, and the evangelized does most of the listening. The further to the right you move, the conversation is much more balanced; there is give and take. On the far right, the talking and listening actually are reversed: the evangelized does most of the talking, and the evangelizer does most of the listening. Thus, what the evangelizer does say is even more poignant and penetrating because comments are focused on what the other person has transparently shared.

Presentation and conversation:
On the chart's far left, what is said is a presentation. On the left hand side, it is all verbal and there are usually a lot of words. However, even here, "all communication should be clear—not clever."[18] On the chart's far right, a conversation takes place. Most of what occurs is nonverbal communication, much like the first means of communication we utilized when we entered this world.

The expected and the unexpected:
Again, on the far left, the encounter is usually scripted, that is, it follows a pattern for presentation centered on Scripture. On the far right, the encounter is much more free-flowing and unformatted. This is in contrast with the far left, where the encounter is

one-sided—any questions asked by the evangelizer are usually to facilitate the presentation, not to engage the individual in conversation. By contrast, on the far right, questions are usually posed by the evangelized who is trying to understand why the believer lives and thinks the way he or she does. The evangelizer asks questions because he or she wants to know the other person as a person and to understand his or her needs. Questions on the left are fact oriented. Questions on the right are feeling oriented.

Invitation to decision or to further discussion:
The encounter on the left side of the chart always ends with a challenge to make a decision about Christ right there on the spot. On the far right, the encounter usually ends with the expectation on both people's parts to meet again, often more than once. I have heard it said that the best form of closure is to keep the conversation open, and people operating in the styles on the right side of our chart would heartily agree.[19]

Salvation as sudden or gradual:
As a result of the kind of invitation discussed above, the salvation of an individual on the far left of the chart is considered as a point in time. On the far right, a person's salvation is a process, an eventual outcome after a long period of engagement and interaction with several individuals besides the main point person. There is truth in the statement, "We are not God's only influence in a person's life."[20]

The decision on the far left comes because of reason. On the far right of the spectrum, the decisions come because of what evangelizers say with their lives and not just with their lips. The evangelized hears the value and validity of the message and makes a decision out of respect. The right-hand side lives out the words commonly attributed to Francis of Assisi (1181–1226): "Preach the gospel all the time, and if necessary, use words."

Information and experience:
On the far left, the focus is about sharing information (what I need you to know). On the far right, the focus is about shared experience (you need to know what I need). In another context, it is like the shift from sales to customer service.[21] I would say it is a shift from information (which can be dispensed in minutes) to influence (which occurs over an extended period of time).

One last observation: personalities transcend ethnic and cultural boundaries. They are all-inclusive and all non-exclusive. No one style of evangelism is better than another. It takes all of them to relate fully to the diverse population that lives within our world today. Though there are specific nuances, the styles are inclusive of all cultures, and all people find themselves somewhere on the spectrum. Personalities are transferable across cultural boundaries. Practices are not.[22] Having said that, we must never allow our understanding and use of methods to take away our dependence upon the Holy Spirit. The early church experience, from which we glean each of our examples, existed in a multicultural world, but the Holy Spirit used people's personalities. People were able to share the Good News according to how they were wired by God. Rather than compete with or contradict their efforts, their personality styles complemented their attempts to share the gospel. While there is truth in the common evangelistic proverb "The only failure in sharing your faith at all is not to share your faith at all," the frustration comes when one tries to share one's faith through a style that does not complement one's own personality.

So let's take a closer look at what those personalities are.

Reminder: if you haven't already done so, please go to Chapter 8 and take the Personal Assessment before reading the rest of this book!

NOTES
1. William Carr Peel and Walter Larimore, MD, *Going Public with Your Faith* (Grand Rapids: Zondervan, 2004), 77.

2. Heather Kirk-Davidoff, "Be My Witness?" *Off the Map*, 2005, http://offthe map.com/idealabs/articles/idl0507-3-witness.html.

3. Ibid. Another attorney said being a good witness meant:
1. being in the right place
2. being in the right place at the right time
3. being at the right at the right time for the right length of time
4. seeing the right things
5. being able to relay what was seen with accuracy
6. the life lived prior to the experience
7. not being paid for one's testimony.
Brenda Salter McNeil, *A Credible Witness: Reflections on Power, Evangelism, and Race* (Downers Grove, IL: InterVarsity Press, 2008), 24.

4. Win Arn and Charles Arn, *The Master's Plan for Making Disciples* (Grand Rapids: Baker Books, 1998), 52.

5. Bill Gilliam, "The White Paper" (Aurora, CO: Training Network for Disciplemaking Churches, 2005), 1. www.tnetwork.com/WhitePaper.htm, accessed May 22, 2009.

6. *Your Church on Mission with God*. Newsletter. June 2007. (Alpharetta, GA: North American Mission Board, SBC).

7. R. Larry Moyer, *Larry Moyer's How-to Book on Personal Evangelism* (Grand Rapids: Kregel Publications, 1998), 70.

8. Steve Sjogren, David Ping, and Doug Pollock, *Irresistible Evangelism: Natural Ways to Open Others to Jesus* (Loveland, CO: Group Publishing, 2003), 55.

9. The *extrovert vs. introvert* idea is advocated by Mike Bechtle in *Evangelism for the Rest of Us* (Grand Rapids: Baker Books, 2006). Those who promote four styles are Jard DeVille, *The Psychology of Witnessing* (Word Books, 1980); Helen Boursier, *Tell It with Style* (Downers Grove, IL: InterVarsity Press, 1995); Greg Stier, *Last Chance: A Student Survival Guide to End-Times Evangelism* (Chicago: Moody Press, 2003); Marita Littauer, *Your Spiritual Personality* (San Francisco: Jossey-Bass, 2004); Joe Aldrich, *Lifestyle Evangelism* (Portland, OR: Multnomah Press, 2006); and Mels Carbonell, *Uniquely You in Christ* (Blue Ridge, GA: Uniquely You Resources, 2006), which makes use of the DISC temperament analysis. Tony Cupit, former Director of Evangelism for the Baptist World Alliance, says there are twenty different models (styles) but doubts even with that number that every biblical model of evangelism has been explored. See Tony Cupit, *Biblical Models of Evangelism* (Falls Church, VA: Baptist World Alliance, 1997), 4.

10. I have come to these six styles with several substyles, adapting the work of Lon Allison (Evangelism and Church Department staff person for the Evangelical Covenant Church in the 1990s), of Mark Mittelberg and Bill Hybels in *Becoming A Contagious Christian* (Grand Rapids: Zondervan, 1994), and Randy Becton in *Everyday Evangelism* (Grand Rapids: Baker Books, 1997). What I found was these authors make a point of stating the styles but not of substantiating them

or of providing evaluation tools for determining them. Some provide biblical examples for each style, while others do not.

11. Jim Petersen, *Living Proof: Sharing the Gospel Naturally* (Colorado Springs: NavPress, 1988), 27.

12. Becton, 56.

13. Ibid., 19.

14. Joseph Aldrich, *Lifestyle Evangelism: Learning to Open Your Life to Those Around You* (Portland, OR: Multnomah Press, 2006), 52.

15. Boursier, 16.

16. Ibid., 73.

17. Michael Green, *Sharing Your Faith with Friends and Family* (Grand Rapids: Baker Books, 2005), 10.

18. Steve Sjogren, et al, 39.

19. Quoted by Harold Percy, *Good News People* (Toronto: Anglican Book Centre, 1996), 126.

20. Becton, 22.

21. Michael Bechtle, *Evangelism for the Rest of Us* (Grand Rapids: Baker Books, 2006), 139.

22. Bruce Dreisbach, *The Jesus Plan* (Colorado Springs: WaterBrook Press, 2002), 136.

CHAPTER 2

the assertive style, or
"this is the way I see it"

If you speak, you should do so as one speaking the
very words of God. If you serve, you should do so
with the strength God provides, so that in all things
God may be praised through Jesus Christ.
(1 Peter 4:11, TNIV)

As described in the last chapter, we have pointed out two broad
categories of Christian servants described by the apostle Peter. Let
those who speak, writes Peter, realize God provides the words. Let
those who serve realize God provides the strength. In both, God is
to be praised. Therefore, we are looking at two basic personality
groups and how God uses them. There are those who engage life
and convey experiences by using their heads; their reality could be
called *word-based*. Others engage life and convey experiences by
using their hands; their reality could be called *work-based*. Chapters 2 through 4 will deal with word-based styles; Chapters 5
through 7 will examine work-based styles. (However, I want to be
clear here: work-based styles do not mean that our works bring
about salvation. These works are good deeds done in order to introduce people to Jesus Christ.)

In thinking about evangelism, three main personality styles emerge
from the word-based reality. I refer to these three styles as *assertive*,
analytical, and *storytelling*. We will examine the assertive style here;
the next two chapters discuss the analytical and storytelling styles.

The Assertive Personality Style

The first and perhaps most intense personality style is the assertive style. Assertive personalities engage life with a verbal directness that some people may consider outspoken at the least. Assertive people tend to be competitive, confident, bold, decisive, and direct; they have very definite, often passionate, opinions. Being task- and goal-oriented, they avoid and even detest small talk. To non-assertive personalities, they may seem bossy, pushy, and insensitive. They can be demanding of themselves and others. They often make emphatic statements without explanation or justification and often won't take no for an answer. They are constantly engaged. Often ignoring social boundaries, they passionately pursue their positions by lecture, argument, or correction. Sometimes without considering the possible consequences, they are completely candid and truthful with friends, even if that truth hurts. Though there may be an intentional desire to speak that truth in love, their emphasis is on the truth, or at least on their perception of it. For better or worse, these personalities make impressions on us precisely because they *are* assertive.

I have found most traditional methods of evangelism to be assertive. Those sold on these methods have told us that we should tell everyone the same thing in the same way because this method works *for everyone*. Tony Cupit adds that often evangelism has been narrowly defined as telling others by word of mouth about Jesus Christ.[1] That might be true if everyone were alike, but all people *aren't* alike.

Pros and Cons of the Assertive Style

As with every personality style, the assertive style has both positives and negatives. Perhaps because the assertive style is at one end of the spectrum, its negatives are most dramatic. Let me share two examples of the negative aspects of the assertive style, one from everyday life and one specifically related to evangelism. You can probably think of several of your own!

A couple of years ago, my wife and I were shopping for a new car, her *first* new car. After spending the morning test-driving several cars and gathering as much information as possible, we were done for the day. I told Kenny (not his real name), the salesperson taking care of us, that we were going to lunch and were going to allow our two small children to burn off some energy in the restaurant's play area. But Kenny didn't want to lose us before winning the sale, so he offered to order food in. We were definitely ready for a break, however, and I declined the offer. He tried another approach. Handing me ten dollars, he said, "It is lunchtime, isn't it? Would you folks pick me up a combo meal and bring it back?" By hook or by crook, Kenny was determined to get us to return. He would even buy us lunch to give us more time to talk about the sale. Kenny really seemed invested in us—until we came back a week after we purchased the car to pick up some additional paperwork. He did not even remember us, because his purpose—the sale—had been accomplished. It did not surprise us to hear that he made head salesman in record time. By one measure, he was good—very good.

Note the similarities between our experience with Kenny and a story shared below by Steve Sjogren and David Ping.[2] It is the epitome of a "spiritual hit and run" that takes assertive-style evangelism to the extreme of aggressive evangelism or evangelism that evokes an aggressive response.

A couple of very zealous Christian students noticed a frazzled-looking husband and wife sitting in a car that had a flat tire. (The couple happened to be non-Christian friends of Steve, one of the authors above, with whom he had been sharing his faith over an extended period of time.) As the students walked up to the car, the more extroverted of the two said something like this:

"Hi, we see you have a flat tire." After pausing for dramatic effect, the student went on. "Did you ever stop to think what would have happened if you'd slammed into that telephone pole over there and had been killed when your tire blew?" After pausing once again to let that grisly image sink in, he inquired, "If you'd died, do you think you would have gone to heaven or hell?"

Though nearly speechless with the shock of their mishap and what they perceived as an unprovoked evangelistic assault, the husband reined in his temper long enough to mumble something like, "Thanks for your concern. Please don't worry about us." With that, the young men abruptly walked away, no doubt thinking they'd given the unfortunate couple some deep spiritual truth to chew on. Sadly, though, their deep concern for the couple's eternal destination did not include enough compassion to offer any help with changing the flat tire so they could get to their temporal destination! It seems to me these students' actions risked turning this couple away from God.

Both my experience with the car salesman and this story of the two students point out the less-attractive qualities of the assertive personality, especially as they relate to evangelism. Assertive people are often gifted verbally at guiding a conversation in order to get people where they want them. When the person responds clearly in one way or another (yes or no), the assertive person then immediately moves on to the next prospect, dare I say, target. Maybe that is why this style, more than any other, uses the phrase "winning people to Christ" to describe evangelistic efforts. Thus, sometimes for the assertive personality, the issue is more about the conquest than the conquered, the contest (of wills) than the convert, about being right rather than helping someone become righteous. I am not saying this is necessarily a conscious effort as much as it is simply evidence of how the assertive personality is wired.

Because of the perceived battle and contest, the assertive style often uses terms that imply a conflict: "commandos for Christ" or "soul-*win*ner." Evangelist Bill Fay's own website states that his goal is to "raise armies of soldiers" willing to share Jesus without fear! Author John Ezekiel says, "We are an aggressive army that goes forth in aggressive compassion, aggressive faith, and aggressive obedience to forcibly advance the Kingdom of God."[3] Church planter Tom Clegg balances this stance by reminding us, "the unsaved aren't our enemies; they're prisoners of the Enemy."[4] The potential faults in this one style are clear, especially for those on the receiving end who are *not* assertive personalities. People can be repelled by the messenger instead of drawn to the Message. "Few more serious mistakes are made in witnessing than memorizing a canned presentation."[5]

The caution here, as with every style, is *never* to manipulate a conversation. Framing the encounter and conversation is one thing. Manipulating it is entirely another. When we manipulate, we act as if the outcome is really dependent upon us. Manipulation shows a lack of respect for the other person as well as a lack of faith that God will do God's part of the work. Jesus guided conversations in order to inspire people to deal with issues in their lives. Jesus never manipulated or misled people; Jesus always left room for them to make their own decisions.

Obviously, the negatives in the assertive personality style are clear, and we have all experienced them. If you are reading this and you are not an assertive-style person, you are probably saying, "Yes! Amen, brother!" *But the positives of the assertive style are also compelling.* Probably more than any other style, the assertive personality is used by God to bring to fruition the previous efforts of various other Christians to lead a person to Christ. Assertive personalities are often used by God to get people to come to a place of decision in a way no other personality style seems to be able to do. Precisely because they are assertive, this personality's gift is to be willing and able to "seal the deal." It should also be noted, however, that very, very few people make a decision for Christ because of one single encounter. Usually, a person who comes to faith in Christ through the efforts of the assertive personality style is able to look back over his or her spiritual shoulder and see a number of seemingly unrelated contacts and connections that God used to bring them to a place of commitment. We cannot say assertive personalities have more skills; often they just have more drive.[6] They are the "closers" among personality-based evangelists!

When we look at assertive people, they evangelize in any of three different substyles: public-assertive, personal-assertive, and phenomena-assertive evangelism.

Public-Assertive Evangelism

This style is called *public-assertive evangelism* because it happens when one person stands before many people and in some verbal way shares the gospel. It is something that you cannot do in hiding or incognito. It is always centered in Scripture, often follows a pre-determined format, and culminates in a challenge to make a decision.

Acts 2 offers us an example of the public-assertive evangelism style. Peter starts his message with questions to engage the crowd, but he seems to expect no responses. Then, he weaves in parts of the Hebrew Bible and brings the message of salvation up to the day of Pentecost, showing the continuity of God's work in people's lives. Peter's message centers on Jesus, why he gave his life, and what the people need to do about it. Peter ends by inviting his hearers to make a faith commitment to Christ. This is the traditional pattern for the assertive style. It is a one-time encounter that is calculated in minutes, no more.

It is important to note here that this encounter, leading to a faith commitment, was between Peter and a large, multicultural group of strangers from all over the world. It included people from every known country and continent on the face on the earth. The people shared a common religion but came from different regions. God used a public-assertive evangelist to birth the first church, and the first church was born out of an evangelistic meeting.[7] The birth of the church was a multicultural evangelistic experience.

Probably the most famous contemporary example of public-assertive evangelism is the recently retired Billy Graham. Standing in front of thousands of people (strangers) in a stadium, Billy Graham's style was to present the gospel in a compelling way entirely through the use of words. Although just about everyone in the stadium would know about Graham, Graham himself would know only a handful in attendance. People knew his name and something of his ministry of traveling around the country verbally presenting the Good News in large-scale, crusade settings. Although Graham's crusades used all the technological advances of the day, his message and methodology remained unchanged. If you watch old broadcasts of his crusades from the 1950s and 1960s, you will note that the only things that change are the color and length of his hair and the style of his suits. Billy Graham preached from John 3 more than any other chapter in the Bible, considering it to be the Bible's paramount passage about salvation. [8] In minutes, the message was presented and an invitation was provided.[9] Actually his invitation often took longer than his message. Both message and invitation were always rooted in Scripture. This method is still as relevant and as effective today as in any era of the church.[10] I believe, though, that today its effectiveness depends on the circumstance and place.

Consider the ministry of Billy Graham as an example. Although his message did not change over the years of his active preaching, Billy Graham was very good at making it connect to the communities where he spoke. He often referenced a broadcast he had heard on the local radio or television station, mentioning the station's name, or cited an article from a local newspaper, thereby establishing greater rapport with people. He connected his message to his audience by tapping into the world in which they lived. Graham was simply following the Bible's expression of assertive public evangelism found in Acts 2.

On the day of Pentecost, Peter stood up under the inspiration and direction of the Holy Spirit and preached before a crowd of many thousands. We can deduce this because when Peter challenged the people to become followers of Jesus Christ, three thousand individuals responded. To be clear: Peter did not get a 100-percent positive response. Jesus didn't either. Jesus was the master of operating within all of the styles, but people still walked away from his offer of new life.

As a teenager growing up in the Pittsburgh area, I practiced this kind of public-assertive evangelism. I would go to a busy street corner, arriving about ten minutes before the bus was scheduled to pick people up at the end of the workday or for a weekend shopping trip. Knowing people waiting for the bus would be a captive audience, I presented the gospel by distributing tracts and quoting one verse after another, emphasizing in those few minutes that they needed to make a decision. Standing there on the corner at my young age, it never failed to amaze me that as I told people that they were going to hell, they would often tell me nearly the same thing! I do not think that we would construe what they said as evangelistic, but they said it with as much passion and sometimes with as much volume as I did. What I did not understand then was this: "Preaching to the masses will never suffice [completely] in the work of...evangelism."[11] Public-assertive evangelism does have an important role to play in sharing Jesus with others, but it is *not* the only—or even the primary—style within this style and among other styles.

Personal-Assertive Evangelism

The second substyle of assertive evangelism is personal. It is the same as public-assertive evangelism, except this substyle involves one-on-one encounters instead of one person speaking to many people. The biblical example is Philip in Acts 8—a great example, because in the earlier portion of chapter 8, we find Philip, the disciple-deacon, speaking to large crowds in Samaria (public-assertive evangelism). Now we find him at the end of the same chapter speaking to just one person (personal-assertive evangelism). This second account clearly demonstrates the intrinsic value God Almighty places on the individual human soul. Though crowds draw the attention of many,

God still focuses on the one. Every crowd is the sum total of individual people.

A North African governmental official was headed home after having been to Jerusalem where he had gone to worship (Acts 8:27). At the same time, God touched Philip on the shoulder and whispered, "I want you to head in this direction. You have a divine appointment!" So Philip headed south into the desert, led by the Spirit of God. It often seems that assertive individuals, more than any of the other personality styles, believe that they are led by the Holy Spirit of God at certain times to certain places to speak with certain people. True as that may be, I believe the Holy Spirit leads people in *all* the styles of evangelism; that leading of the Spirit is just more obvious in some styles than in others. The encounter between Philip and the public servant occurs in the desert, symbolic, from the assertive perspective, of spiritual barrenness and desolation.

From verse 27, we learn some important things about the Ethiopian. He was a man of status and means. He was a secretary of the treasury of Ethiopia, under the authority of Queen Candace, and thus had great authority and influence. We notice also that he was reading a scroll as he traveled, which indicates something about his wealth because (1) to be reading while riding he must have been chauffeured and (2) in that day to possess a copy of the book of Isaiah in scroll form would have cost a considerable amount of money. He was most likely a God-fearer, following the Jewish religion. We know this Ethiopian was a eunuch, and under Old Testament law, this physical circumstance prohibited him from full participation in Judaism. Verse 27 gives us a picture of an upstanding, brilliant, powerful, and prestigious person.

In light of all this, we can see two important things: First, we discover Philip offered this Ethiopian the opportunity to make a faith commitment. Philip was a layperson, not a clergyperson, and new—as they *all* were—to the Christian faith. I want to emphasize this because evangelism is not just for "professionals."

It's for anybody! You don't have to be long in the faith to share your faith.

Second, this passage points out the Ethiopian's need. Here we have Philip encountering this person who, by the world's standards, has it all together. He is wealthy, educated, well traveled, and influential; he has a personal spirituality and a corporate religion. However, God's appearance in this narrative demonstrates a spiritual need in the eunuch that only God could supply. What Philip offers to this man is what he is lacking—a personal relationship with God through a faith commitment to Jesus Christ.

And that is why the Lord sent Philip his way.

Acts 8 tells us that after Philip pointed out selected Scriptures, he brought the message around to Jesus Christ. There is a need to do so in both the public- and personal-assertive styles of evangelism. Philip began his evangelistic encounter by asking questions (v. 30), did most—if not all—the talking (v. 35a), led the Ethiopian through Scriptures (v. 35b), and directed the conversation, one-sided as it might have been, to Jesus (v. 35c).

A great contemporary example of the personal-assertive style of evangelism comes from Randy Hurst, who was director of evangelism for the Assemblies of God and the author of the book, *Response Evangelism*.

In his denominational role, Randy travels a lot. He said that once, during a ninety-minute airport layover, he decided to get his shoes shined. Having made flight connections in that airport over two hundred different times and having had his shoes shined there often, he noticed the stand always had a waiting line and two to four workers. But on this particular day, only one other man came at the same time Randy did. Randy arrived at the stand first, but since his flight was a little later than the other man's, Randy allowed him to go first. After the other gentleman left to catch his flight, Randy was there with the lone shoe shiner. As they conversed, Randy asked about his family. The shiner explained that he was divorced because of his wife's repeated unfaithfulness. Even after Randy's shoes were shined, they continued to talk. During this whole time, no other customers came to the stand. Randy asked about the man's spiritual life and told the fellow about God's plan for his life, explaining this plan could not happen unless he was in a right relationship with God through Christ. After their brief conversation, Randy asked the man if he was prepared to invite Jesus Christ into his life and offered to pray with him. The man said yes. So Randy put his hand on his shoulder and led him in a prayer to accept Christ into his heart.[12]

Randy pointed out that he becomes "spiritually suspicious"— that is to say, *sensitive*—when he is in circumstances where, normally, other people would be around, yet he finds himself alone with someone.[13] Where most people would be even more withdrawn in such a one-on-one encounter, the assertive-style person finds clear motivation to share Christ.

In the above story, you see all the basic elements of the personal-assertive methodology:

- Occurs between two strangers (Randy and the shoe shiner)
- Begins by asking questions often about general things in life (How is your family?)
- Conversation is maneuvered towards spiritual things (How is your spiritual life?)
- Conversation centers around Scripture
- Results in a challenge to make a decision
- Encounter lasts only minutes[14]

The chief contemporary proponents of this methodology include the late Dr. D. James Kennedy, creator of Evangelism Explosion. His is probably the most famous personal-assertive evangelism program ever produced and has been used to lead thousands, perhaps millions, to Christ. It begins with these questions: If you died today, where would you go? If you showed up in heaven and God asked why you should get in, what would you say? Then one verse after another is presented in a scripted way in order to lead a person to a point of decision. Dr. Kennedy extrapolated principles he had learned in his BC (before conversion) days as an award-winning Arthur Murray dance instructor, and he applied them to evangelism. He grew a church of only fifteen people into a congregation of more than twelve thousand.

Many of these methodologies came out of the post-war era, when American society was still open to "cold contact" evangelism, as seen in the methods of Billy Graham *(Peace with God)*, Bill Bright of Campus Crusade for Christ *(The Four Spiritual Laws)*, and Dawson Trotman of The Navigators *(The Bridge)*. More recently, Bill Fay shares the same content (but with nowhere near the success rate) as these earlier people. (To see what the presentations among assertive styles have looked like over the years, see Appendix C for a chart.)

It is easy (and even humorous!) for me as an ABCUSA pastor and national executive to share with you the classic A-B-C method of sharing the gospel. As with the above examples, what follows can be found in nearly every publication that deals with evangelism. What Stan Toler advocates is below (and this is probably similar to how Paul would have presented it):

A: Admit you are sinner (see Romans 3:23)

B: Believe Jesus died for you (see John 1:12)

C: Confess with your mouth that Jesus is your Savior
(see Romans 10: 9-10)[15]

Toler continues by saying that a "trainee's" first step is to memorize the order of the presentation[16] and then describes what assertive personalities obviously consider a biblical script:

- Ask (evangelizer)—starts with a question
- Answer (evangelizer)
- Response (evangelized)
- Answer (evangelizer)
- Response (evangelized)
- Ask (evangelizer)—ends with a challenge[17]

Assertive personalities are great at providing a structured, very systematic message; for some, it is all they feel the need to offer. It is pretty much a one-size-fits-all presentation. It begins with a question and ends with a challenge. Questions are intended to engage a person but not to get the person's answer. The presentation can be made in minutes; some evangelists say it is designed to be short enough to share during an average elevator trip. The content is rooted in Scripture; explanation, justification, or interaction is not the goal. Often the vocabulary is highly religious—*saved, born again, redeemed*—terms Jesus did use, although only with religious audiences.

A noted weakness of this personal-assertive evangelism style involves the motivation for the use of methods such as door-to-door calling or its counterparts (tract distribution). Although the successes of either effort are very few[18], the deeper concern is that the assertive-style person often assesses personal spirituality in terms of how often and how successfully a person has shared his or her faith. Canvassing communities in order to get people into a local church—instead of getting Christ into people—can easily become the motivation for the personal-assertive person.

Please don't misunderstand! The presentations or formats provided above or in the appendix are not wrong. They all merely point to the existence of the assertive style. That approach is easy to identify because it *is* assertive. This style is alive and well and still very much needed.

Phenomena-Assertive Evangelism

Acts 5:12 states that the early church leaders performed many miraculous signs (words) and wonders (works) among all the people. As a result, verse 14 states that more and more men and women believed in the Lord and were added to their number. This event refers to the third substyle of assertive evangelism, what I call phenomena-assertive evangelism. Phenomena-assertive evangelism has not commonly happened in church history.[19] Mark Stibbe notes, "Most of their modern [charismatic] experiences don't see many salvations but are part of a process that can 'nudge' people closer to God."[20]

More often than not today, this third substyle is found within the Charismatic as well as Pentecostal traditions, which are more theologically receptive to these experiences, but it is not exclusive to them. Most trace the modern expression of this substyle to the Azusa Street Revival in Los Angeles in 1908.[21] The Los Angeles revival had its roots in the 1904 Welsh Revival, during which approximately one hundred thousand people in Wales converted to Christianity. Internationally, evangelical Christians took this event to be a sign that biblical prophecy in Joel 2:23-29 was about to be fulfilled. Joseph Smale, then pastor of the First Baptist Church in Los Angeles (an American Baptist church), went to Wales in order to personally witness the revival. Returning to Los Angeles, he attempted to ignite a similar event in his own congregation. His attempts were short-lived and not well received. Leaving First Baptist Church in 1905 to found First New Testament Church, his continuing efforts led to the Azusa Street Revival.[22]

Prophetic-Assertive Evangelism The third substyle of assertive evangelism actually has two subtypes. The first subtype is prophetic-assertive evangelism and involves miraculous information. It's the kind of information about another person that couldn't possibly be known unless God whispered it in your ear or spoke it to your spirit. A prophetic word in general can speak to the person's past, present (forthtelling), or future (foretelling), all three, or in some combination. It literally can be insight or foresight. When these revelations occur, they create faith in both the evangelized and the evangelizer. Prophetic-assertive evangelism can speak to someone's harbored hurts or secret sins that are revealed by the Holy Spirit to the evangelizer. It can take the form of God giving a believer words of knowledge (unknown information) or wisdom (unknown instruction). Sometimes God works directly with the non-Christian in dreams and visions. The purpose of prophetic words is sometimes to challenge and bring conviction, sometimes to bring affirmation, and sometimes to bring confirmation that God knows who a person is.[23]

If we return to the story of Peter and Pentecost, Act 2 states that prior to Peter's preaching, those assembled believers were filled with the Holy Spirit (v. 4) and began to speak languages the disciples did not individually know but that were known by the individuals in the crowd. God miraculously used these many languages to attract interest, causing people to pay attention to what Peter had to say. Peter then shared the words of the gospel in a universally understood language, very possibly Greek, which was the *lingua franca* of the day. God gave his disciples the ability to speak many languages, making this encounter culturally relevant and very personal.

I remember the account of a pastor who received a phone call late one night. On the other end of the line was a woman he did not know. She said she intended to commit suicide. As they spoke, the pastor's mind raced, trying to remember all the things he had been taught for moments like this, but none proved useful. So the pastor began to pray. He did remember that you needed to get the person's name in order to form some type of human connection. But, the woman just wouldn't share her name. After a few more minutes, she said, "I didn't call for you to try to convince me not to do it." That response was exactly what he was trying his best to prevent! He frantically tried to remember anything that might be helpful, but he was reduced to repeating Christian bumper stickers and little spiritualized clichés. *Nothing* made a connection with her.

They both sensed that the conversation was coming to an end. There wasn't much more to say. The woman finally said, "Listen, I just called because I wanted someone to know I decided to do this, not out of desperation but, rather, determination." She saw no other way to deal with the realities of her life. She said, "Well, I'm going to go now." The pastor was terrified that she meant that statement in the ultimate and fatal sense. He could hear her voice fading as she prepared to hang up the phone.

Suddenly, the pastor said, "Helen (not her real name), don't hang up that phone!"

He could hear the phone come back to her ear, and she asked, "What did you say?"

The pastor responded, "Helen, don't hang up this phone."

There was a pause. Then she asked, "How do you know my name?"

The pastor continued, "I didn't know your name, but God does. He didn't create you for this."

They agreed to meet. They talked together about her situation. He shared about salvation through Jesus Christ. She made a faith commitment to the Lord and is alive today. How did this pastor know Helen's name? A lucky guess? No. The Holy Spirit marvelously, miraculously gave the pastor her name.

Power-Assertive Evangelism A second subtype of phenomena-assertive evangelism is power-assertive evangelism and involves miraculous action. This is where God does something that someone can touch or see. God touches the person in the physical realm to connect with him spiritually. While prophetic-assertive evangelism is God speaking through words, power-assertive evangelism is God speaking through tangible actions or outcomes.

This type of evangelism is exemplified in Acts 9 in the account of Saul's conversion. As we mentioned earlier, Saul vigorously persecuted the Christian church. Believing that Christian Jews were heretics, he felt it was his God-ordained responsibility to rein them back into the true faith or to end their spiritual infection in the Jewish body. With murder on his mind, he headed to Damascus (v. 2), but then he had a dramatic encounter with Jesus Christ. "Apparently the early church considered Saul a hopeless case…Jesus had to witness to him personally."[24] Afterward, Saul sat for several days in physical and spiritual darkness.

Acts 9:10-11 tells us God tapped on the spiritual shoulder of a Christian believer named Ananias and said (in so many words), "I want you to go and speak [that's the verbal part] to a man named Saul." Ananias replied, "The only Saul I know is persecuting Christians." God said, "That's the one." Ananias probably responded with something like, "Well, I obviously will be seeing you soon, God!" Despite his fears, the Lord directed Ananias to go to the place where Saul was and to share the Good News. When Ananias laid hands on Saul, "something like scales" fell from Saul's eyes, and he regained his sight (v. 18). Saul was able to see—physically *and* spiritually! Just as in Saul's case, God uses physical healing in the lives of not-yet Christians to get their attention; in getting their attention, God then opens them up to verbally hearing the gospel.

There is clearly a risk factor for people involved in phenomena-assertive evangelism and its subtypes. It moves Christian and non-Christians alike out of their comfort zones. Some move easily, but most do not. At best, Ananias gave God a halfhearted yes. But God doesn't need you to be in the best of attitudes to be used. The presence of and dependence on the Holy Spirit is more evident and important here than in other styles. These events are by divine arrangement; they seldom occur on our schedule or timetable. Only God could set up something like Ananias going to Saul or the pastor knowing Helen's name. God puts people together in situations they never could orchestrate themselves to bring someone to faith in Christ. As you start praying for divine appointments, be ready to receive the oddest calls, to find yourself in the strangest meetings, and to be part of the most surprising conversations, all of which happen at the most inopportune times.[25]

The Assertive Personality Style in a Nutshell

Okay, let's pull this all together and put this all in perspective. Statistics provide some revealing insights about how many people come to church, though not necessarily to faith in Christ, through the formal methodologies of the assertive-evangelism style:

- Church service or evangelistic program: 3 percent
- Personal visitation, door-to-door calling: 2 percent
- Evangelistic crusade or TV/radio program: 0.05 percent [26]

Because of the isolated time and insulated culture in which we live, these statistics now will probably be lower, not higher.

Here are two additional statistics. Only 5 percent of all Christians have ever shared their faith with another person (presumably through assertive methods).[27] Of those in attendance at any Billy Graham crusade, only 5 to 7 percent make a spiritual decision.[28] Is it then realistic to think that everyone who claims the name of Christ does so because of the assertive-evangelism style? This seems unlikely. If you aren't a part of the 5 percent of the Christian population who has found faith through someone's assertive methods, by the efforts of evangelists, or through those with the gift of evangelism, then there are other means by which people come to a personal faith in Jesus Christ. I reject the idea that faith comes only through the assertive-evangelism style.

Remember, there is only way one to God: through a personal faith in Jesus Christ (John 14:6). The verse's structure makes that clear when Jesus says, "I'm it; besides me there is no one else and no other way." However, there are many ways *to Jesus* and many ways to share the story of Jesus. There is no one correct way. Author Michael Green said there are a rich variety of ways.[29] People experience conversion (living for Jesus instead of living for self) in different ways, depending on their environments, their emotional needs, their spiritual backgrounds, and the Holy Spirit's work in their lives.[30] Therefore, "different people respond to different approaches."[31] Most of the rest of this book deals with these other styles that help people find those ways to Jesus. Though we do not cook like we did fifty years ago, drive what we drove fifty years ago, or watch TV like we did fifty years ago, we still fall back on modern-era evangelistic methods to reach a postmodern world. I believe there is one message that never changes, but there are many methods that are always changing in order to be both relevant and contextual. No one approach fits either the giver or the receiver of the gospel. There's one right message, but no one right way to present it.[32] The most effective churches, and by extension, the most effective Christians, are those who understand the different types (styles, as I put it) and how to maximize for evangelistic purposes.[33]

"If ordinary church people are to become excited about evangelism, they must be offered models that do not require them to act like highly extroverted lobbyists."[34] That is what the rest of this book is about—ordinary people excited by evangelism that fits them, not frustrates them.

NOTES

1. Tony Cupit, *Biblical Models of Evangelism* (Falls Church, VA: Baptist World Alliance, 1997), 3.

2. Steve Sjogren and David Ping, *Outflow: Outward-Focused Living in a Self-Focused World* (Colorado Springs: Group Publishing, 2007), 120-121.

3. John Ezekiel, *Miracle Evangelism* (Fawnskin, CA: Powerhouse Publishing, 1996), 55.

4. Tom Clegg and Warren Bird, *Lost in America: How You and Your Church Can Impact the World Next Door* (Colorado Springs: Group Publishing, 2001), 135.

5. Jard DeVille, *The Psychology of Witnessing* (Dallas: Word Books, 1980), 74.

6. Helen Boursier, *Tell It with Style* (Downers Grove, IL: InterVarsity Press, 1995), 78.

7. Cupit, 5.

8. Lon Allison and Mark Anderson, *Going Public with the Gospel* (Downers Grove, IL: InterVarsity Press, 2004), 39.

9. Allison and Anderson, 116.

10. Allison and Anderson, 44.

11. Robert Coleman, *The Master Plan of Evangelism* (Grand Rapids: Revell Books, 1994), 40.

12. Randy Hurst, *Response Evangelism* (Springfield, MO: Access Publishing/Gospel Publishing House, 1995), 67.

13. Hurst, 73.

14. In *31 Days with the Master Fisherman* (Grand Rapids: Kregel Publications, 1997), Larry Moyer says it takes about fifteen minutes to lead a person to Christ, which assumes the Assertive Style. In contrast, Win and Charles Arn note in their

book *The Master's Plan for Making Disciples* (Grand Rapids: Baker Books, 1998) that such an encounter does not take into consideration the needs of the individual. Peel and Larimore, in *Going Public with Your Faith* (Grand Rapids: Zondervan Publishing, 2004), contend such encounters are unwise at the least, if not flat out unethical. I would not go as far as that judgment.

15. Stan Toler, *ABCs of Evangelism* (Kansas City, MO: Beacon Hill Press, 2002), 11.

16. Toler, 54.

17. Toler, 13.

18. In their book *How to Talk about Jesus without Freaking Out* (Portland, OR: Multnomah Press, 2001), authors Jim and Karen Covell and Victorya Rogers estimate that for every ten people who say they hate the impersonal nature of tracts, one became a Christian because of reading a tract. I would personally question such a high ratio. I have heard that one in three hundred accepts Christ from reading a tract, but the ratio increases to one in one hundred if a person reads the tract with a Christian.

19. Mark Stibbe, *Prophetic Evangelism* (Colorado Springs: Authentic Publishing, 2004), 13.

20. Stibbe, 16.

21. Ezekiel, 18.

22. Gary McGee, "William J. Seymour and the Azusa Street Revival." Assemblies of God USA *Enrichment Journal* (Fall 1999). http://enrichmentjournal.ag.org/199904/026_azusa.cfm.

23. Stibbe, 62.

24. Scott Wilkins, *Reach: A Team Approach to Evangelism and Assimilation* (Grand Rapids: Baker Books, 2005), 117.

25. Covell, Covell, and Rogers, 74.

26. Arn and Arn, 46.

27. R. Larry Moyer, *Larry Moyer's How-to Book on Personal Evangelism* (Grand Rapids: Kregel Publications, 1998), 65.

28. Allison and Anderson, 119.

29. Michael Green, *Sharing your Faith with Friends and Family* (Grand Rapids: Baker Books, 2005), 140.

30. Duncan McIntosh, *The Everyday Evangelist* (Valley Forge, PA: Judson Press, 1984), 60.

31. George Barna, *The Habits of Highly Effective Churches* (Ventura, CA: Gospel Light Publications, 2001), 117.

32. Allison and Anderson, 164.

33. Barna, 117.

34. Harold Percy, *Good News People* (Toronto: Anglican Book Centre, 1996), 66.

CHAPTER 3

the analytical style:

or "I think, therefore I am."

Let's look back at the assertive style for a moment. As we have seen, fewer than 3 percent of Christians evidence that style and exercise it evangelistically. Yet, we often emphasize the assertive style because that style fits what is perceived to be the most successful method of evangelism, at least in terms of numbers. This might be because people in the assertive style are quite vocal. Some are able to articulate their positions so loudly and long—so assertively!— that many of us have come to believe it is the only style just because they have told us this is so.

In biblical terms, individuals who exercise evangelism under the assertive style would certainly be designated as evangelists. But the work of evangelism is not limited to assertive practices. There are other ways to lead people to Jesus Christ! To see this clearly, just ask a group of church people, "How many of you came to faith in Christ through a mass meeting, a crusade, or a tent revival? How many became Christians because of a television program, a radio broadcast, a door-to-door calling program, a one-on-one witnessing encounter, or something similar?" You'll find only one or two people in one hundred, almost always older adults, who made a faith commitment as a result of such activities. And that's a maybe.

I want to repeat an important conclusion from Chapter 1. *Unless* those two or three people out of one hundred are the only truly saved ones (despite all these other people who have been in church for years), then God uses other ways—and specifically other styles of evangelism—to bring people to faith in Christ! Simple facts and figures show that there must be more ways to evangelize than those used by people who score high under the assertive style. If there aren't, then almost all of us are lost, in more ways than one.

The Analytical Style

One of these other ways to evangelize is found in the analytical style. Here we're looking at individuals who see the world in a logical, commonsense way. They're inquisitive, often well educated (maybe even the most educated of all the styles), and, well, *analytical!* Avid readers and online surfers, they know what's going on in the world. They enjoy discussions about controversial issues. They enjoy debating topics and issues. They take nothing at face value. They like to solve difficult problems. They may be list makers. They process things. They are methodical and take their time making decisions. They are cautious and conservative in their choices. They weigh the pros and cons. They get frustrated with people who use weak arguments, and they like to dig into the underlying reasons why people hold certain opinions and beliefs. Circumstances for them are the sum total of all facts and figures. They may even make a literal list on paper of the positives and negatives of an issue. The world for them is very structured and organized, even if their lives or workspaces are not!

Occupations that appeal to this personality style are ones that engage the world in terms of facts and figures. Included here are chemists, accountants, architects, engineers, researchers, and economists. These people emphasize academics. For that reason, I also identify college professors—at least the ones whom we remember more for what they taught than just for who they are. The analytical style of evangelism is needed today because clearly we live in an analytical age. Of all the scientists who have ever lived, 90 percent are alive and working today.[1] The analytical style has also been referred to by some as persuasion evangelism, in that we provide convincing reasons for what we believe and why another should also believe. However, in this particular case, it is not the method of persuasion but the information itself that is important. A typical attitude among those with the analytical style is found in the words of Christian apologist, theologian, and author Clark H. Pinnock:

> I am convinced that faith needs to face up to the truth question and that the Christian message fits the facts. It is not a presupposition that has to be accepted on authority or a self-evident truth that needs no argument; it is a solid truth claim that can be tested and verified across the whole range of human experience. It meets our existential needs, makes sense out of our religious institutions, stands up under rational scrutiny, corresponds with the historical evidence, and speaks to today's moral necessities...Act upon the evidence that stands before you.[2]

Note that where the assertive personality tends to operate under the assumption that the gospel is a "self-evident truth" to be accepted without debate, the analytic personality, like Pinnock, believes that *because* the gospel is true, it should be questioned, tested, and debated. Only through such testing can faith be put in terms of the world as the analytic personality understands it.

Pros and Cons of the Analytical Evangelism Style

As with all the personality styles, there are positive and negative aspects with the analytical approach. On the positive side, analytical personalities are perceptive, inquisitive, thirsty for knowledge, and accurate about information gathered. They are able to organize many ideas and concepts, capable of understanding instructions, and committed once the process or task makes sense to them.

Imagination plays a huge role here. Because the analytical personality style is inquisitive and curious, life is not as cut and dried as it is for the assertive personality, yet not as colorful as that of the storyteller (as we will see in Chapter 4). Analytical personalites are the people we admire for being able to see through a situation and verbalize clearly the heart of a matter.

On the other hand, when the dark side of the analytical personality comes out, it is skeptical, resistant, inflexible, and opinionated. They are often slow to make decisions. Sometimes they avoid choosing, even allow events to make the choice for them. In those cases, they find themselves reacting to life rather than proactively engaging it. Occasionally when they do make decisions, those choices are based on a priori concepts instead of empirical existence and experience. How does this relate to evangelism? It is an insight to keep in mind should the person you are attempting to share the gospel with respond with skepticism or resistance or reluctance to choose Jesus. It may take an analytical personality to engage and convince another analytic!

Curiously, some characteristics of analytical personalites can be classified as both positive and negative. For example, analytical personalites make lists, either in their minds or on paper. This is positive, because they can balance out different views. But the negative aspect is that they overanalyze and procrastinate in a decision, because for them the facts may never add up exactly. Another group of positive/negative characteristics are introspection, reflection, and contemplation. The positive side is that analytical personalities can do all these things very well in relation to facts and figures; but on the other hand, reflection about emotional issues or content is too messy and often avoided. Similar to these traits is the ability to focus. Analytical personalities can tune in completely to what is being said; however, they can focus so exactly on a singular point, they miss the forest for one tree. Analytical personalities can be meticulous in attention to detail about some things and literally messy about others. Albert Einstein was one of the most noteworthy analytical personalities, untangling the mathematics of the universe, yet needing copious help to keep his papers and writings in order. One result of the analytical person's meticulous methods, however, is that this personality tends to produce our most articulate and prolific Christian apologists—individuals adept at laying out the evidence for our Christian faith.

Paul: The Analytical Style in Action

One biblical example that shows the analytical style in action is in Acts 17:1-4, where Paul encounters the people in the synagogue at Thessalonica.

> When they had passed through Amphipolis and Apollonia, they came to Thessalonica, where there was a Jewish synagogue. As his *custom* was, Paul went into *the synagogue*, and on three Sabbath days he *reasoned* with them from the Scriptures, *explaining* and *proving* that the Christ had to suffer and rise from the dead. "This Jesus I am proclaiming to you is the Christ," he said. Some of the Jews were persuaded and joined Paul and Silas, as did a large number of God-fearing Greeks and not a few prominent women [italics added].

Notice the analytical words in this passage, italicized here. It was Paul's *custom*, that is to say it was Paul's habit, his bent, his practice. Analytical personalities like patterns and routines. Verse 2 identifies the place as *the synagogue*, a place of higher education, and there he *reasoned*. Verse 3 builds on that by saying he *explained* and *proved*. The outcome was that people were persuaded (v. 4). Why? Paul's gospel argument made sense to them. In a Greco-Roman culture that prized logic and learning through questioning and debate, these people weighed the content of Paul's message, and most found it acceptable and agreeable with their own reasoning.

Paul's own description of himself in Philippians 3:4-6 further demonstrates his analytical style.

> ...though I myself have *reasons* for such confidence. If anyone else thinks he has *reasons* to put confidence in the flesh, I have more: circumcised on the eighth day, of the people of Israel, of the tribe of Benjamin, a Hebrew of Hebrews; in regard to the law, a Pharisee; as for zeal, persecuting the church; as for legalistic righteousness, faultless [italics added].

At the time of the apostle Paul's ministry, the city of Athens was full of intellectual people. In Acts 17:16-33, Paul has traveled to Athens and has walked around. Paul doesn't just show up in this Greek community and start preaching in the public forum. He spends the day walking through the city, connecting with the heartbeat of the people. Who lived there? How did they live? What did they believe?

The men who escorted Paul had brought him to Athens and then had left with instructions for Silas and Timothy to join Paul as soon as possible (v. 15). While Paul was waiting for them in Athens, he was greatly distressed to see that the city was full of idols. So he reasoned in the synagogue with the Jews and the God-fearing Greeks, as well as daily in the marketplace with whoever happened to be there. A group of Epicurean and Stoic philosophers began to dispute with him. Some of them asked, "What is this babbler trying to say?" Others remarked, "He seems to be advocating foreign gods." They said this because Paul was preaching the good news about Jesus and the resurrection, new ideas and events for these people. Then they brought him to a meeting of the Areopagus, a legal council of Athenian citizens, where they said to him, "May we know what this new teaching is that you are presenting? You are bringing some strange ideas to our ears, and we want to know what they mean" (vv. 19-20). This was a typical invitation. All the Athenians and the foreigners who lived there spent their time talking about and listening to the latest ideas. Scripture records Paul's encounter with these analytical people as such:

> Paul then stood up in the meeting of the Areopagus and said: "Men of Athens! I see that in every way you are very religious. For as I walked around and looked carefully at your objects of worship, I even found an altar with this inscription: TO AN UNKNOWN GOD. Now what you worship as something unknown I am going to proclaim to you.
>
> "The God who made the world and everything in it is the Lord of heaven and earth and does not live in temples built by hands. And he is not served by human hands, as if he needed anything, because he himself gives all men life and breath and everything else. From one man he made every nation of men, that they should inhabit the whole earth; and he determined the times set for them and the exact places where they should live. God did this so that men would seek him and perhaps reach out for him and find him, though he is not far from each one of us. 'For in him we live and move and have our being.' As some of your own poets have said, 'We are his offspring.'
>
> "Therefore since we are God's offspring, we should not think that the divine being is…an image made by man's design and skill. In the past God overlooked such ignorance, but now he commands all people everywhere to repent. For he has set a day when he will judge the world with justice by the man he has appointed. He has given proof of this to all men by raising him from the dead."

The entire passage is quoted here so you might clearly see several important things. First, evidently Paul was acquainted with the culture and context of Athens. He acknowledged the existence and significance of the temples, statues, and other symbols of culture in this community. Second, he did not look down on the Athenians as inferior. They represented the intelligentsia of Greco-Roman society, and Paul respected them as such. He did not accept their worldview, but he honored it nevertheless. Third, he stood up in the public forum, on their turf and in their terms, and shared his faith in a clear, logical way—a way that suited both his own personality and that of many of his hearers: he used logic, reason, and analysis to talk about Jesus. He then allowed the gospel presentation to simmer in his listeners' minds. This was a format Paul employed several times in various locations, as recorded in the remainder of the book of Acts.

This biblical model offers an ideal case study for analytical personalities, but there are valuable lessons about evangelism for all of us. No matter what our personality style, our own evangelistic efforts need to be culturally aware and sensitive. The great barriers to effective evangelism are often not theological but cultural and social. When you walk into someone's home, right away you can get an idea of what really matters to the people who live there. You see pictures on the walls, furniture, and other items that tell you what's important to these people. We also need to remember that, like the Ethiopian eunuch, like the people in Athens, many people who don't know Jesus Christ are socially and vocationally productive, and they share many of the same moral values as believers. The difference— or spiritually speaking, the deficiency—is that they do not have a personal relationship with God through a faith commitment to Jesus Christ. That's where our sharing Christ comes in and is why it is important to cultivate the various personal evangelism styles.

When we speak with analytical people about Jesus Christ, such a person might ask an analytical-style question like, "Can the Bible be trusted?" or "Why do people suffer?" Instead of firing back a quick, scripted response (in the assertive style), it is better to say, "That's a good question. Why don't we both think this over for a while? That will give me a chance to really consider what you've asked." This shows the person that you value her, are really listening to her, and think what she has to say is worth considering. One cannot be ready for every single question that the evangelized might pose. However, using their natural analytical skills, analytical personalities have the skills and wiring to find answers they do not immediately have. As the conversation freely flows—at a very intellectual level in this style—difficult questions are posed. Unlike in the assertive style, the evangelizer here listens and makes mental and/or physical notes to research before the next meeting. When the discussion does take place, DeVille reminds us, it is important to use the word *and* rather than *but* in refuting ideas.[3] Contrasted with the more scripted interactions of the assertive style, the analytical style, as well as those styles that are discussed later in this book, incorporates conversations that are spontaneous, though obviously on different emotional, intellectual, and spiritual levels. The evangelized primarily raises the subjects for further study and discussion. In this and the styles to follow, the evangelized controls more of the conversation, and the evangelizer provides the spiritual content.

A further word about *apologetics* is appropriate here. The term identifies the classic defense of the Christian faith. Many Christian books are really apologetics—reasons why the Christian faith is true, believable, and to be embraced—and these resources tend to be written by analytical people. *Mere Christianity* by C. S. Lewis is one example. But when it comes to sharing Jesus one to one, the approach changes. The *evangelized* determines what needs defending in any given conversation. Even if the evangelizer knows the answers to the questions being asked by the evangelized, returning to the conversation at another time gives the evangelized time to process the spiritual content they have been given. Time to process is very important in this style. Returning for further discussion shows that what the evangelized has said is valued; the ideas were not just dismissed so the evangelizer could make his or her points. Analytical personalities would do well to read much in the area of apologetics in order to be able to engage others in such conversations.

The Time Factor

It is important to note that each successive style adds more high-quality interaction between people—and often takes more time! It is time spent getting to know people and what they value and how they live. Episcopal priest and author Harold Percy says people need ten essential things to understand enough about the Christian faith to give it their serious and informed consideration.[4] I do not agree with that high number, but the need for even a few such essentials obviously means the case for Christianity cannot be presented by the evangelizer nor processed by the evangelized in one short encounter. More time and talking are required than one encounter provides. So as we move from the first style to the second, there will be more than one encounter, though probably not more than a few, especially if the analytical evangelizer does not sense enough movement toward commitment to Christ on the part of the evangelized. This style needs to see a return on their investment of time, logic, and information.

Even though analytical people may not spend huge amounts of time with the evangelized, their discussions do get them involved with people to a limited degree. Willingness to invest some time in others conveys an attitude of availability, and with each successive evangelism style discussed in this book, such an attitude is increasingly important. Our responsibility in evangelism is to share information and experience—both by what we say and what we do—and each takes time. We need to be especially careful that this doesn't turn into a high-pressure sales pitch. Convincing and convicting people is the work of the Holy Spirit. Our job is to make contact, put the Good News on the table, be available to engage seekers further, but ultimately to allow people decide what to do with the gospel. Sometimes, when we get a negative reaction to our efforts, we stop sharing our faith. But remember this: It's the message and not the messenger that has been rejected. Don't take it personally. The way we behave can certainly improve the reception of that information or make its acceptance more difficult. But if we have done nothing offensive in presenting the information, then the response we get is not about us; we need to simply leave it with the Lord. We need to believe that God is more at work in this process than we are, working before we showed up, while we were speaking, and long after we have gone. Emphasis must be placed on the power of the Holy Spirit instead of on our ability of presentation.

The Various Responses

Before we leave the Acts 17 passage, let me highlight another lesson in this text—one that is valuable for all personality styles. In this narrative (as in other biblical passages) people respond in a variety of ways to the message about Jesus. Paul receives three different reactions. These are typical across the spectrum of styles but nowhere more evident than with the analytical style. (Consider, in contrast, the reject or accept duality that the assertive style typically inspires.)

First, some *receive* the message immediately (v. 34). The numbers who react in this way are few, probably because analytical personalities (to whom Paul's method would have strongly appealed) need time to think, to process, to *analyze*.

Second, some in the crowd *request* more information and discussion (v. 32). These folks were saying, "This is good, but let me go home and think about it and get back to you." There is no clear script for these exchanges, so don't be anxious or apologize if the questions that are raised (in the moment or later in a subsequent encounter) are beyond your current knowledge. Offer to study the matter further, yourself, with the questioner, or even by introducing another Christian who has more knowledge of the issue.

The third response to Paul's message comes from those who *reject* the message outright (v. 32). Such rejection can take many forms. Some people, who are analytical types themselves, may try to entrap the person making the evangelistic effort, in much the same way that the Pharisees tried to trap Jesus with a trick question about coins and taxes (Luke 20:19-26). Others will be less confrontational but turn away all the same, like the rich young ruler in Luke 18, who found the cost of discipleship too high.

Assuming that what happens in Acts 17 is typical of responses to evangelistic encounters, the majority of people either want more time or reject the Good News out of hand. We need not be too surprised when this happens to us.

The Analytical Style throughout History

There are several historical and contemporary examples of individuals who exhibited the analytical style. Although not usually thought of in terms of evangelism, Blaise Pascal, the seventeenth-century mathematician, physicist, and religious philosopher, said that though the existence of God cannot be determined solely by reason, God's existence could be calculated in terms of probabilities. In contemporary language, Pascal's analytical, rational argument— Pascal's Wager—goes something like this: If I live my whole life like there is a God, die, and then discover there is no God, I have lost nothing. But if I live my whole life as if there is a God, die, and then discover God does exist, I have gained everything. Based on this analysis, the probability that God exists was very high for Pascal, and he became a believer. His wager appeals to many people who need more than shoulds or oughts in order to come to faith. It appeals to the analytical personalities among us.

Another analytical-style person was the great Baptist missionary Adoniram Judson, who devoted his adult life to the heroic translation of the Bible into Burmese, one of the world's most difficult languages to master. Adoniram's father, pastor of the Third Congregational Church in Plymouth, Massachusetts, had sent him to Brown University with high hopes. Academically, Adoniram had consistently led his class in grades and was an honor student. Spiritually, however, he had gotten into company with Jacob Eames, who was a professed atheist and persuasive unbeliever. Eames's analytical arguments led to Adoniram's total rejection of Christianity.

After graduation, back home in the parsonage, young Adoniram opened the Plymouth Independent Academy. All the while, he played dual roles. On the outside, he piously took part in family worship and church attendance. On the inside, he denounced everything he had been brought up to believe spiritually.

Bored with life in Plymouth, he left home and embraced a vagabond's life. One night, he took lodging in a local inn. Adoniram was tired and needed rest, but rest did not come. Throughout the night, he heard sounds in the next room, mostly the agonizing cries of despair and desperation, obviously coming from a dying man. Thoughts and questions about death haunted Judson's mind and heart. How would he face this enemy, Death? He knew his own father welcomed it as the doorway to God. Judson came face-to-face with the fact that his current philosophy offered no answers.

At sunrise, Judson inquired, "How is the sick man?"

"Dead," the innkeeper replied.

"Too bad," Adoniram replied respectfully. "Did you know him?"

"No," the innkeeper replied. "He was a young man from the college in Providence. He registered as Jacob Eames."

That shocking reality sent Adoniram's mind reeling. He wondered about the eternal destiny for someone like Jacob, a man without hope. Suddenly, he understood that his father's God was true: The beliefs of Jacob Eames, which he himself had accepted, were empty and had failed Jacob at his greatest hour of need. Judson left the inn that morning, headed for Plymouth.

Back home, after weighing the arguments for and against the Christian faith, he was convinced in his mind and convicted in his heart that the Jesus of the Bible was the one and true Way. Committing himself fully to God, he devoted his life to the ministry. Twelve days after his marriage to Ann Hasseltine in 1812, he sailed with his new bride to the Far East, eventually settling in Burma.

After laboring under inhospitable conditions for seven long years, the couple rejoiced in their first convert. Today in Burma, there are 3,905 Baptist congregations with nearly 663,000 baptized believers. This earliest work among the Burmese came through Judson, a man who had found a reason for faith and then used his analytical style to not only share Jesus but to provide the Burmese people with a dictionary, the Bible, and their language in written form.

The Lord has spoken to and through a number of analytical people over the years. Most recently, legal journalist Lee Strobel did a study of "just the facts" concerning the life of Christ from both biblical and extra-biblical sources. Originally his goal was to prove Christianity false. But ultimately, like others before him, he concluded that Jesus is who Jesus claimed to be. Strobel then knew he was responsible to act upon that rational conclusion. Strobel presented his understanding in *The Case for Christ: A Journalist's Personal Investigation of the Evidence for Jesus.* Josh McDowell's *Evidence That Demands a Verdict* and his other works offer yet more examples. Such analytical people consider the gospel in light of solving a problem, making an investigation, answering a question, or trying to prove or disprove a theory. Under the tutoring of the Holy Spirit, they come to Christian belief from a starting point of inquiry, and once the information is laid out and makes sense to them, they make a faith commitment.

I don't think you can find a more definitive description of an analytical testimony than the one provided by Don Bierle, author and president of FaithSearch International: "In my quest for God, I spent several months with numerous lines of excellent evidences. I dialogued with several people. I weighed the pros and cons of a commitment to Jesus Christ. But the time came when I had to ask the question, 'What is the spiritual bottom line?'"[5] For those with the analytical bent, faith is a commitment-making process, based upon the Word of God, and without regard to any emotional questioning of the Word.[6] This style often comes down to an analysis of the classic debate about whether Jesus is a liar, a lunatic, or actually the Lord he claims to be. Given this common line of questioning, "In today's skeptical climate, it is probably best to begin with Jesus' humanity, than His divinity."[7]

As will be mentioned in subsequent chapters, each style plays a complementary role to the other styles, especially those that are right beside them in the layout of the chart (p. 11). Assertives make emphatic and impassioned statements without justification, with the exception of quoting a particular Bible chapter and verse, but even then don't necessarily expound about the passage, but rather let it speak, as they perceive it, for itself. In contrast, Analyticals come alongside and provide the elaboration to these statements and Scriptures.

While Assertives ask all the questions, Analyticals start making a necessary transition to the other styles by beginning to ask questions of their own with an expectation of an explanation. Because within this postmodern culture there are often no absolutes, the Word of God is not seen as the definitive authority that it once was; it is not taken at face value, and it is deemed by some to have no spiritual or societal value. Therefore, Analyticals draw into the conversation historical facts and extra-biblical references that further support the case for Christianity.

NOTES

1. Jard DeVille, *The Psychology of Witnessing* (Waco, TX: Word Books, 1980), 37. Note: This analytical statistic was from nearly thirty years ago. The percentage today is as high, if not higher.

2. Clark H. Pinnock, *Reason Enough: A Case for the Christian Faith* (Downers Grove, IL: InterVarsity Press, 1980), 119, 121–22.

3. DeVille, 114.

4. Harold Percy, *Good News People* (Toronto: Anglican Book Centre, 1996), 115–16.

5. Don Bierle, *Surprised by Faith* (McLean, VA: Global Publishing Services, 2003), 106.

6. Bierle, 79.

7. Michael Green, *Sharing Your Faith with Friends and Family* (Grand Rapids: Baker Books, 2005), 71.

CHAPTER 4

the storytelling style:
"have I ever told you about..."

In the previous two chapters, we have examined the assertive and the analytical word-based styles. In this chapter, we will look at the storytelling style, the third and last style under the word-based styles of evangelism, i.e., doing evangelism primarily through what we say. The storytelling style uses words to create mental images and becomes a transition to the works-based styles on the right side of the styles chart (see p. 11), because of what people hear as well as see. Because often the most effective storytellers are also good listeners, there is more opportunity for everyone involved in the evangelizing experience to share with one another. Storytellers pick up on key points in an evangelized person's story and then shape their own narratives to include connection points and common ground. Duncan McIntosh said, "Good storytelling is best done after good story listening." He defines *story listening* as the ability to hear the truth that others tell us in their stories.[1]

Storytellers are entertaining, engaging people. These folks have a huge vocabulary and love to use all of it—all in one conversation, if possible! They are more vocal, compared to the analytical people. Their verbiage is more descriptive and their gestures more demonstrative. They are full of adjectives and use several in every sentence. They are able to make you feel that you are reliving the experience with them. Every time storytellers recount their life stories or a portion of them, it is as if it is the first time. Storytellers take literally the words of Shakespeare in *As You Like It*, "All the world's a stage, and all the men and women merely players." For storytellers, all the players are supporting cast, except them—they believe they are the stars. It is all about them. They epitomize the classic joke, "Enough about me. Let's talk about you...what do you think about me?" As such, they are people who need people, an audience. Otherwise, with whom would they share their stories? Because of how storytellers are wired, every day is a new chapter and every experience is extreme and intense, at least to them. Life is an unfolding, day-to-day drama. Dr. Emmett Johnson (no relation, but a predecessor in my position within the ABCUSA) said, "Evangelism is done by laypersons who between Sundays best live out the drama of salvation through Jesus Christ."[2]

The Pros and Cons of the Storytelling Style

As we already mentioned, every style has its positive and negative characteristics. Storytelling is no exception. Storytellers need to be careful not to just share their stories and never get to sharing Jesus' story. Never getting to "The Story" happens either because they share their stories in such a way and for such a length of time that either Christ's story is left out or because the evangelized has simply lost interest. The result is that Christ's story has no lasting effect. To guard against this, storytellers should be able to tell the core of their spiritual narrative in less than five minutes. It is recommended that the essence of personal conversion stories last approximately three minutes, because that is the average time one is able to hold a listener's undivided attention.[3] If given permission, we can later elaborate and expand. Storytellers need to avoid stories for stories' sakes and instead be contextual, speaking to the audience who listens.

My brother-in-law, an avid outdoorsman, has shared his faith journey story by relating it to the various calls of turkeys and to the seasons of the year at which their noises change. He actually has perfected the mimic of most, if not all, of them, using that example to convey his personal testimony to other outdoorsmen. He does this in short order but with the kind of enthusiasm that keeps his listeners engaged. We need to find our own stories based on our interests, experiences, education, and lives. The story has to be personal to make it powerful. It has to interest us if it is going to interest others.

The Storytelling Style in Action

Occupations in this style include actors, entertainers, and musicians, to name some major ones. Music is a story put to a melody. Some of the most powerful songs are those that tell a story with which we can connect. In Acts 16, Paul and Silas sing psalms and hymns during their imprisonment. It was this means of conveying the message that woke their jailor, shook the earth, and eventually led to the salvation of the jailor and others. Music is an international, intercultural language. Authors probably fall into storytelling more than any other style. Introverts convey their stories through words that are written, not spoken.[4] The difference between spoken or sung words and written words is the difference between singers and songwriters.

By way of example, author Mike Bechtle speaks of what I call the exponential potential for a writer to touch thousands, if not hundreds of thousands. He relates a personal experience of such potential being realized:

> Years ago, I wrote high school Sunday school lessons for a large interdenominational publisher. Once a quarter, the lesson would include a presentation of the gospel. The curriculum was dated, so I always knew which Sunday the lessons were going to be taught. One Sunday I woke up and did the math. At that time, the publisher's curriculum was being used in about sixty thousand churches across America. There was an average attendance in high school

classes of about ten students. That means that before the day was over, I had arranged for the plan of salvation to be presented to around six hundred thousand high schoolers. Let's say one student out of a thousand actually made a commitment to Christ that day—probably a conservative estimate. If accurate, it would mean that my lesson would have resulted in about six hundred people making a decision for Christ in one day.[5]

Because the story of Jesus is the story of God's intervention in human history, its telling has the potential to attract people's attention and change lives.

The Time Factor

Now that we have moved on to the third style, we find we are engaged with other people for more than just a few minutes. At this place in the continuum, we are talking days of time and multiple encounters, because the storyteller engages a person on more than one occasion. Because stories can be so engaging, the evangelized become more and more transparent. In response, the evangelizer has an opportunity to pick up on these shared cues and begin telling connective life experiences, ones that reveal the believer to be human and real. No one wants to be around someone who is or is perceived to be perfect. All that does is make the imperfect person feel inferior, not receptive. One's vulnerability is more important than one's image.[6]

A biblical example of the storytelling evangelism style is the woman at the well in John 4. It is the longest evangelistic narrative in the Gospel records, and that is one reason I place it under the storytelling style. As with previous examples, note how Jesus exhibits cultural sensitivity in the passage. Evangelism should always take into consideration a person's frame of reference, their cultural, educational, and environmental factors.[7]

In all of the biblical case studies we have considered thus far, we have encountered people with a personal spirituality and involvement in institutional religions. Peter encountered the Jews who were in Jerusalem for the observance of the Jewish feast of Pentecost. Philip encountered the Ethiopian, who had just been in Jerusalem worshipping—as far the limits of his religion would allow him. Ananias encountered Saul, who was so dedicated to his religion that he was willing and even wanting to kill for it. Paul encountered the Athenians who had a statue to every god they could imagine. Similarly in John 4, we will discover that the Samaritan woman at the well questions Jesus out of her pre-existing knowledge of religion.

In the same way, most people we meet will not be in a spiritual vacuum. Every time one of the people or groups presented so far in this book was approached evangelistically, they had some knowledge of or experience with religion, but they lacked the critical relationship with God through a faith commitment to Jesus Christ that makes a person a Christian. Just as in these examples, it is important to start from where people are, spiritually speaking, and not judge their thinking. We can acknowledge a person's beliefs without affirming them.

An Encounter at a Well

After a long walk from Judea, Jesus arrives at the well and sits down. Sitting slows him enough to be available to engage with someone else. His disciples have gone on into town to purchase lunch (v. 8). Jesus' silence and solace are interrupted by a woman who arrives around noon (the sixth hour in Jewish timekeeping) to draw water. Knowing the customs of the culture, Jesus picks up on the fact that she comes at a time when most women do not. This window on the culture is another reason I place this account under the storytelling style. When we deal with societal prejudices like this

woman did—gender, ethnicity, culture, and religious tradition—
we know for sure the person has a story to tell. These societal
biases may be the very reason Jesus decides to encounter her alone,
away from the conscious and subconscious prejudices of his disciples and her community. Fortunately, Scripture gives us a chance to
eavesdrop on their conversation that afternoon.

First we get a look at Jesus' totally human side. Being tired and
thirsty, Jesus sits down at the well. The woman arrives to draw
water. She is alone. This is unusual. For women, the duty of gathering water was traditionally a daily time of communal experience,
catching up on the activities of the night and sharing the plans for
the day ahead. Women normally drew water in the morning for the
day and in the late afternoon for the night. It seems this woman
had not gone that morning, hours earlier when all the other
women went. Jesus does not need any supernatural insights to pick
up on the simple fact that in a culture where women do nearly
everything together, she is there alone and at a time when other
women are not.

Her solitary appearance coupled with the cultural norms lead to
two possible observations. First, something may have happened to
prevent her from coming that morning, or she has come at noon because she knows something is going to prevent her from coming
later to draw water. The second possibility is that she may not want
to be with the other women—or they may not want to be with her.
In any case, Jesus sees there is something not routine here. Scripture
does not indicate the woman is surprised to find a man at the well,
just taken aback that he speaks to her (v. 9).

I point all this out to highlight the fact that somehow the daily
routine is disrupted for her. All these probabilities indicate that
through circumstances or choice, something is not right in her life.
Knowing that, Jesus has a divinely appointed moment with her.

Another important fact in this story is that Jesus encounters the
woman on her turf. Although the unfolding conversation might

have been unfamiliar to her, the location was where she went every day, usually a couple of times a day. Their conversation begins with Jesus' request: "Will you give me a drink?" (v. 7). He starts with something they share in common, his need of water and her ability to provide it. She replies, "How can you ask me for a drink?" (v. 8), knowing that the culture prohibits it. A man was not allowed to speak to a woman in public (prohibition of gender), and Jews did not speak to Samaritans (prohibition of geography and culture).

Historical background is necessary here in order to fully understand the power of Jesus' encounter with the Samaritan woman. Various foreign powers had controlled Israel throughout the latter half of Old Testament times and had transplanted people from their own countries into conquered Judean territories, so they would mingle and even marry the indigenous folk. These conquered people now had inherent or inherited connections with the conquering power; thus, any potential uprising was squelched or at least suppressed. The decisive blow of alienation came when these Samaritans offered their services to Ezra and Nehemiah to rebuild the Jewish temple in Jerusalem. Their offer was refused because of their perceived racial impurity, and both Jews and Samaritans developed different cultures over the ensuing years.

So when Jesus encounters the Samaritan women, he encounters a person considered by Jewish society to be inferior: She is female, a Samaritan, and adheres to an adulterated religion. Jesus' use of the storytelling style bypasses these prejudices. This may well be the first cross-cultural evangelistic encounter in the New Testament.

Being sensitive to the culture but also in conflict with it, Jesus speaks with this woman who was considered a second-class citizen (as were all women in that day). He treats her with respect, though undoubtedly others did not. After the first exchange (vv. 9-15), Jesus then does what is still required in some Middle Eastern countries today. Acknowledging it is socially improper for a man to speak publicly to a woman who is not his wife, Jesus tells her, "Go, call your husband and come back" (v.16). The mandate of the day was that the woman's husband be present or grant permission for such a conversation to occur. Her reply is, "I have no husband" (v. 17), absolving Jesus of this cultural responsibility. And so the conversation continues.

The Importance of Listening

Notice that even though Jesus is privy to personal information about this woman and knows everything about her, Jesus lets her speak and actively listens to what she says. Jesus affirms what she says by saying to her, "You are right when you say you have no husband" (v. 17). Here Jesus operates within the prophetic assertive style of evangelism by revealing information that would not otherwise be known unless it came by a supernatural source. He presents this information without justification or explanation. He provides the information because she does not voluntarily offer it up. Who of us would?

Jesus demonstrates by his responses that it is important to actively listen to what people are saying. A person may tell you something, but not everything. It has been said that "the reason why we have two ears and only one mouth is that we may listen more and talk the less."[8] I like to say that we have two ears and one mouth so we will listen twice as much as we speak. This kind of listening is an essential part of the storytelling style.

Jesus multiplies the impact of his statement by adding, "The fact is, you have had five husbands, and the man you now have is not your husband. What you have just said is quite true" (v. 18). Now imagine how this affected her. What was racing through her mind, as her heart rate increased? Again, taking some clues from the culture of the day, we can only speculate about her past. She may have been divorced; she may have been five-times widowed. In either case, by the fifth husband, the culture would have looked askance at her, considering her used property or cursed with bad luck. Most people would have viewed her with suspicion or disdain. That reality would explain why this woman is not present during the usual times for drawing water. Some of the other women could have been the spouses of the men with whom she has had immoral relationships.

Whatever the specifics of the woman's history, she has suffered a great deal of loss and she is currently alone. It seems probable that she is lonely because she has not found lasting satisfaction for her life. At the very least, we can conclude this woman is a seeker, looking to belong, looking for love, but perhaps seeking in all the wrong places and from all the wrong people.

What we can say for certain is that this woman has a story; given the culture, it appears everyone knows it. Verse 39 says many Samaritans believed because of the woman's testimony (story), telling them, "[he] told me everything I ever did" (v. 29). She has a testimony that others know and her words confirm. Again, we assume there is more to the conversation than is recorded here, but what is here is sufficient to show us a changed life.

It is important to note the woman's response. By touching on her relationships, Jesus hits a nerve—and she hits the road, intellectually speaking. She attempts to divert the conversation in a very different direction. She deflects focus from herself to the age-old question of which religion is the right religion. She asks Jesus where he thinks people should worship. The Samaritans had their holy site, and the Jews had a different one. That is the equivalent of today's argument, "What church is correct?" or "Which religion is the true religion?" Jesus immediately maneuvers—but not manipulates—the conversation back to the matter at hand, saying, "What is important is a relationship with God, not religion" (vv. 23-24). When engaging people at this level, we may encounter such diversions when their stories reveal some kind of pain. This kind of conversation is very personal. Conversion is very personal. They go hand in hand.

The Importance of Transitions

Looking at how Jesus starts where the woman is, we see that transitions are critical. Jesus moves from what was essentially small talk related to their immediate setting (asking for a drink from the well) to casual invitation (go get your husband) to deeper spiritual conversation (theological questions about worship). Sometimes the transitions emerge quite naturally out of the circumstances for us. Jesus uses the metaphor of living water while talking next to a well and sharing a refreshing drink. Other times we have to create transitions for ourselves—rather like Philip did by asking the Ethiopian if he understood what he was reading.

Just as transitions are important in the way we talk with people, so transitions are important in the way we walk with people. As people experience significant changes and different crises in their life stories, they become more receptive to the gospel. Needs often create an open door spiritually, in the lives of others. Nearly 50 percent of people come to faith in Christ through need or crisis.[9] So people on both sides of the styles chart must be intentionally sensitive to these transitions.

If we look at the whole narrative from John 3 and 4, there is a striking contrast. In John 3, the epitome of a righteous or religious person (Nicodemus) meets with Jesus at midnight because of a need (and was disparaged for coming at night). In John 4, the Samaritan woman tries to meet her needs at midnight in the arms of all these men. The turning point for the woman at the well happens after Jesus' conversation with her and she goes back to town, leaving behind the water jar. In the first century, a water jar was a clearly valued possession. She leaves it behind because she has found something even more valuable: a relationship with Jesus.

To some degree in all the styles, we talk about the idea of relationship: building relationship horizontally as the conduit to introducing people to a relationship that is vertical, between them and their creator God. What we have is the woman leaving behind her water jar, running back to town, and telling the people, "You've got to come out and meet a man who told me everything I ever did" (v. 29). Note that she starts by saying, "Come." It is a word of relationship. It is a word we hear over and over again throughout the Bible: Don't just go; let me journey with you. She does not just send the townsfolk to Jesus. She goes with them to make the introductions personally. Their willingness to come seems to rest in part on the fact that they know about her story. Now she is inviting them into her story. The willingness to be engaged happens as more time is spent together in a shared experience. Consider how in this story the evangelized is transformed into an evangelizer! That is the ultimate engagement with the gospel story.

The Importance of the Story We Tell
There are many levels of storytelling in this chapter of the Bible. On the one hand we have the disciples. In this story, the disciples have been in town themselves, but the Scripture doesn't mention that *they* bring anyone out from the community to meet Jesus. Don't you wonder what kinds of stories the disciples were telling—or not telling—while they were in town? On the other hand, Jesus uses storytelling to reach the woman. In turn, the woman uses storytelling to reach her community and context. Thus, the story ends with a response to the woman's story. She uses her story to get them to come meet Jesus. I can picture the whole town turning out to meet "the man." She knew many men, but for some reason this one stood out from all the rest. Undoubtedly, she has never introduced any of her other men to the community. She does not have to; the community would have known who those men were. If the woman has been in unacceptable relationships, I have to wonder if there weren't a few men running ahead of the rest of the people and asking her, "Did he mention any names? Did this man specifically mention mine?" To be sure, some of the townspeople came out of curiosity, but undoubtedly there were others who came because

they thought if this guy could do something for *this* woman, he certainly could do something to meet their needs.

The community goes out at the woman's request to meet Jesus. Then they invite Jesus to stay with them, which he does. Jesus' impromptu willingness to stay two whole days speaks to the need to be available in this whole evangelistic experience. It would take me (and probably most of us) three whole months to open up that much time on the calendar, because we are just too busy. But the results are clear. When Jesus is ready to leave, the townsfolk say, "We were challenged to come out and meet you because we know this woman and her story." She uses storytelling to bring them to Christ. The people respond by saying, "We have been changed because we heard you [Jesus] for ourselves" (v. 42).

The Importance of Belonging

Before leaving our discussion of the story of the woman at the well, we need to note one more thing. This story emphasizes the importance of *belonging* before *believing*. Just as the woman lets people in on her whole story, we need to let people get close to us before they make a faith commitment to Christ. This relational factor will have a more primary focus as we move to the final three styles. In these styles, we draw people in to journey along side us in order that they can see the truth in the gospel being lived out in us before they make a faith commitment.

The Storytelling Style throughout History

The power of story is strong because we are wired for stories. Every generation has its storytellers who connect the Good News to people. In 1678, John Bunyan wrote the first part of *Pilgrim's Progress,* finishing the second part in 1684. It is probably the most famous Christian story in allegory form ever written and has never been out of print. In fact, after the Bible, the second book missionaries often translate into an indigenous language is *Pilgrim's Progress.*[10]

This book tells the story of Christian, an everyman type of character, who makes a journey from his hometown—the City of Destruction (or this world)—to the Celestial City (or heaven). The book tells of the trials, temptations, and help he receives along the way. Though not formally educated, Bunyan had a clear, compelling style of storytelling, making him wildly popular in his day. Today we would say he had a bestseller every year from 1678 to his death in 1688. His works widely influenced both Christians, non-Christians, and literature in general.

Another person who used the storytelling style to share the gospel was John Newton. Before his conversion, he had spent much time trying to drink away the pain and stain of his slave-trading work. After Newton came to faith in Christ, he was moved by the Holy Spirit to write his testimony in song to a tune sung in the pubs and bars of the day. We know that story today as the song *Amazing Grace.* In this music, we have a story, written down, and put to music—all three components in the fullest form of storytelling.

This century has been influenced widely by such storytellers as C. S. Lewis and Max Lucado. Lewis, similar to Bunyan, uses allegory in his best-known series, *The Chronicles of Narnia,* to describe the Christian faith and journey. Author of picture books like *The Crippled Lamb* and adult inspirational titles such as *Facing Your Giants,* Lucado uses story to make Christian truths accessible to children as well as adults.

The Storytelling Style in a Nutshell

We are meant to be a storied people. Spoken language precedes written language, in history and in childhood development. Before there were books, there were storytellers and troubadours who transmitted human history orally. There are still cultures who share learning and life experiences primarily through the telling of stories. Of all the people in the world, 70 percent rely on stories, drama, song, poetry, and chants to learn.[11] The storytellers, more than any other style, give us personal testimony of coming to faith in Christ. A personal testimony is the most non-threatening way to introduce a person to Christ. We can use personal testimonies to tell unbelievers why Jesus is important to us. Our stories are compelling because they show how Christ changed or continues to change our lives. We can prove the story is true because we were there! It can't be refuted.[12]

However, we need to be clear about the role of stories. A person's story does not save other people. A person's story is God's vehicle used to convey God's story, which is the means of salvation. This is especially true for those called *Generation X* (culturally defined as born after 1960). Author and speaker Leighton Ford says that narrative evangelism is the key to reaching the hearts and minds of Generation X.[13] They live their lives by stories (with music as their primary expression of story), so the storytelling style is an important way to connect with today's younger adults in sharing the Good News. The interconnectedness of this style with the next two styles will be discussed in the next chapters.

A final word about testimonies. An effective testimony has three basic components: a BC time (Before the testifier met Christ), an EC moment (the testifier's encounter with Christ), and an AC time (After Commitment to Christ), when the testifier is clearly changed by Christ for the better. A testimony should avoid negative talk about other people. A testimony should contain at least one verse of Scripture and should mention the name of Jesus, because our lives as Christians are about our personal relationship with God through Christ.

Biblical examples of testimony offer further insights. We are not told any of the particulars of the Samaritan woman's story, probably because her people already knew it, but also so as not to glorify the wrongs she had done. In Paul's testimony in Acts 26, there is a brief introduction (vv. 2-2), a time before he met Jesus (vv. 4-11), the way he met Jesus (vv. 12-18), and an experience since he met Jesus (vv. 19-22). Duncan McIntosh, said "you should build the habit of at least weekly focusing on some specific experience in which the presence and the power of God were especially real to you...By keeping this record of God's work in your life, your story remains current."[14]

Contrary to popular thought, one's testimony doesn't have to be dramatic to be effective. Actually, the more ordinary the better, because that is where most people will find a connection. These stories are not uninteresting to people! "God simply doesn't write boring stories."[15]

NOTES

1. Duncan McIntosh, *The Everyday Evangelist* (Valley Forge, PA: Judson Press, 1984), 22.

2. McIntosh, 6.

3. Jim and Karen Covell and Victorya Rogers, *How To Talk about Jesus without Freaking Out* (Colorado Springs: Multnomah Press, 2001), 108.

4. Michael Bechtle, *Evangelism for the Rest of Us* (Grand Rapids: Baker Books, 2006), 83.

5. Bechtle, 83.

6. Covell, Covell, and Rogers, 29.

7. Bill Hull, *Jesus Christ, Disciplemaker* (Grand Rapids: Baker Books, 2004), 55.

8. Attributed to Benjamin, Earl of Beaconsfield Disraeli in *Henrietta Temple,* book vi, chapter xxiv. www.bartleby.com.

9. "What Brings People to Jesus in New England?" *Vision New England: A Study of Some 200 Recent Converts* (Northborough, MA: Baptist Convention of New England, 2009), http://www.bcne.net/evangelism/personal-evangelism/what-brings-people-to-jesus-in-new-england-200.html (accessed May 1, 2009).

10. "John Bunyan." *Wikipedia.* http://en.wikipedia.org/wiki/John_Bunyan (accessed March 17, 2009).

11. Gary D. Foster, compiler and editor, *Mission America Coalition Evangelism Connection,* March 2009. http://web.memberclicks.com/mc/getLink.do?id=74324104113696241381IBD1P&linkId=4647 (accessed March 19, 2009).

12. Covell, Covell, and Rogers, 100.

13. Ibid., 184.

14. McIntosh, 18–9.

15. Harold Percy, *Good News People* (Toronto: Anglican Book Centre, 1996), 107.

CHAPTER 5

the relational style,
or "thank you for being my friend."

As we move into the next style, we make our transition from the word-based personality styles of evangelism (assertive, analytical, and storytelling) to the works-based styles of evangelism. I remind you that the three final styles are based upon the latter part of 1 Peter 4:11, which says, "If anyone serves, he should do it with the strength God provides, so that in all things God may be praised through Jesus Christ." These next three styles are found in individuals who do evangelism more effectively by what they do, rather than by what they say. They utilize their hands more than their heads, works over words. Again, I want to be clear: Although I am using the term *works,* I do not mean that works lead to salvation. Works are good deeds done after salvation to help others come to Christ. As we move from left to right on the styles chart, it is important to note that the right side represents a larger portion of the message and a greater portion of the people who share the message. Words alone carry only about 7 percent of any message. Some 55 percent is communicated through nonverbal means—body language and body action—leaving 38 percent of the message to be communicated by the tone of voice.[1]

As we look at the relational style, it is important to refer back to the style chart (p. 11) and look at the lines of separation between the styles. These are not carved in stone. (Only the Ten Commandments were!) Though there are individual lines drawn between all six styles and an even thicker and longer line between the two broad categories, these lines do not represent impermeable walls. Think of them as dashed lines, because in reality and experience, these styles blend and meld together. In addition, even though you are looking at a linear chart, please recognize that life is not that compartmentalized. There is a free flow among the styles, and a meshing of personality styles occurs more often than not in an individual who has a primary and secondary style. The styles come together, completing the person and enabling the individual to be used by the Holy Spirit in his or her evangelistic efforts, complementary to his or her personality styles. For example, when it comes to the relational style, being a good friend means listening; being a good storyteller also means listening. Thus there is an inherent connection between these two styles. There are similar connections among the others styles as well.

Also, as we move into the three personality-based styles of evangelism, each one has a specific orientation, a direction in which people focus their energies. The style we discuss in this chapter is a people-oriented style, and we dub this focus *relational*.

Relational individuals are available, trustworthy, attentive to others, transparent, connective, and very loving. They are genuine, sympathetic, unconditional, nonjudgmental, and patient. They believe in shared experiences. All these qualities are true across all the three of these works-based personality styles, but the emphasis for relational-style people is the emotional connection. These traits are often found in people in the helping professions, such as counselors, psychologists, psychiatrists, therapists, chaplains, and teachers.

Here I want to contrast the relational style with the analytical style, where we found people in occupations such as engineers and professors. We often do not remember college or graduate school professors as people, partly because none of us had much time for personal, relational interaction with our instructors. Although personal relationships can occur (especially if the school is small), we most often remember professors because of what they taught us—

the facts and the figures, the content and information. We might even remember them because we understood what they were trying to teach us! On the other hand, we most often remember our grade school teachers—not because they taught us to read, write, add, and so forth. We remember them for their relational characteristics: They were kind, caring, encouraging, and helpful on many levels. Their sense of connection is often so strong that they remember us long after the classroom years.

To illustrate the power of relationships, let me share a personal story. A couple of years ago, I had the opportunity to tour one of our American Baptist schools of higher education. As my guide walked with me through one building, she stopped at a professor's office to ask a question unrelated to my visit. While they were conversing in the doorway, I happened to glance into the professor's office and saw hanging on his wall a photo of the mascot of a professional sports team—and it was not a local team. When their conversation ended, I said to him, "You are either a transplant from another community and have brought your hometown team loyalties with you, or if you are from this community and have that mascot on your wall, you have a death wish." He replied that he actually had grown up in a small town on the other end of the state. "You probably have never heard of it," he said. I responded, "You might be surprised. In my role, I travel all over the place, so if I haven't been to it, I have probably been through it, and for sure have been close by it."

Now this professor was some thirty years my senior. We had never met before. Just as he was ready to tell me the name of his hometown, he turned his head in such a way that I was mentally transported back in time some thirty years. Have you ever had an experience like that? A sight, a sound, a smell that triggers memories that have long lain dormant, that you didn't even realize you still retained? Before the professor could say anything, I asked him if his last name was *Muse*. He spun around in his doorway and looked me straight in the eye and said it was. Before he could continue, I asked if his mother's name was *Millie.* He said, "Yes, but she has been gone for almost—" and I finished the sentence, "—thirty-some years." He was stunned. I explained with tears in my eyes that not only had I known his mother, but she had been my earliest Sunday school teacher. She had been the first person I could remember in my life who told me that God loves me. That one woman's ministry of introducing this young boy to Christ still continues to impact thousands today, nearly four decades later. I really do not remember anything this woman specifically taught me in that little Sunday school class. But the relational connection made week after week between teacher and student changed a little kid forever. The power of one life can be replicated through the lives of others.

The Relational Style in Action

One clear biblical example of this relational style is found in the first chapter of the Gospel of John. Here we find Philip the disciple-apostle (in contrast to Philip the disciple-deacon we examined in connection with the assertive style in Chapter 2). In John 1, Jesus calls his first disciple, Andrew; subsequently, Jesus calls Andrew's brother, Peter, through Andrew. Then we find Jesus in Galilee, approaching a man named Philip. The text says Jesus "found Philip" (v. 43), indicating Jesus is intentionally on the lookout for this fellow. He finds and invites Philip to follow him. Here again, we find the element of multiculturalism. From what is said here, we know that Philip is a Jew. But *Philip* is a Greek name, which tells us he was probably the son of a multicultural marriage: one parent was Jewish; the other parent, Greek. Philip is connected to both the Jewish part as well as the Greek/Roman part of the ancient world.

After making the decision to follow Jesus, Philip immediately goes and shares his encounter with Nathanael (v. 45). Here is another cultural nuance. Since Nathanael's name is provided without distinction of location (like his hometown), lineage (his parents or grandparents), or titles, we realize Philip and Nathanael know one another personally. The lack of titles used in reference to either of them indicates the relationship between Philip and Nathanael is one of friendship. Now note, this life-changing encounter with Jesus Christ does not lead Philip to undergo immediate training, nor does he immediately start a 501(3)c non-profit itinerant evangelistic organization. Rather, he immediately goes and finds a friend—someone with whom he has had a long-standing relationship of trust built over time. On this foundation of respect and trust, Philip shares this great news that has enhanced his life and would do so forever. Though Philip has no guaranteed outcome as a result of his efforts, he knows Nathanael as a person whom he trusts and who trusts him. Philip believes Nathanael will believe what he has to say. Similarly for us, when we experience something wonderful in our lives, we probably do not call strangers to tell them about it. We certainly do not go get training about how to tell others about it. We just share that wonderful news with those who are closest to us, and we know how to reach them. Philip, too, knew where to find his friend.

So Philip finds Nathanael. From both his name and the ensuing conversation, we understand Nathanael is probably an observant and educated Jew. His very name speaks to the Jewish religion. The *el* of his name is the Hebrew name for God. Philip approaches Nathanael and says, "We have found the one Moses wrote about in the Law, and about whom the prophets also wrote—Jesus of Nazareth, the son of Joseph" (v. 44).

Let's pause here and again look at this relational component that is often overlooked. It comes to light in the early earthly life of Jesus. In the first century, Nazareth was a town in the Galilean part of Israel, an agricultural segment of the country. I read once it was a community that comprised about seven acres with a resident population of about 150. As such, everybody knew everybody and probably knew everything about everybody, too! The chance that someone of significance would come from there was statistically small. Jesus was raised in that town—one smaller than most towns the readers of this book come from. Although the Gospels share very little of the first three decades of Jesus' life, there is no indication Jesus ever felt his life in that very small village was a waste of his time. And yet during the vast majority of those years—ten times the length of Jesus' public ministry—he lived in relative obscurity. Jesus devoted himself to those 150 people for thirty years and never once regretted a moment of it. There is no hint in the Gospels that Jesus did any miracles or gave any teaching that caused people to be attracted to him. And yet, once Jesus began his public ministry, we find no less than three and possibly as many as five times that his own immediate family came and asked him to come back home. It was not because he provided food, healed all their sick, or shared insights they had never heard before. It was simply because of who he was and the relationships he shared with them.

People often say that Jesus' public ministry began when he turned the water to wine in John 2. But that emphasis allows the miracle to overshadow the significant relationships that preceded it—the connections with Andrew and then Peter, and with Philip and then Nathanael. Even the marriage event itself—one of the most significant relational events of life—stands out because two families come together and form a new family with a potential of an even greater family. The most significant element of the story of the wedding at Cana is not Jesus' changing water to wine. The most important part is that he shows no hesitation whatsoever in changing lives. That is the real miracle. Jesus invests himself in plenty of relationships and then expects those relationships to be extended to others through the faith commitment of those who come to him.

The relational component here in John 1 makes a very important point. In every person who comes to saving faith in Jesus Christ, God sees the potential salvation through Christ of yet another person. This in no way diminishes the value of any person's commitment to Christ. What it does say is that in one saved life, God sees the possibility of more: Andrew and possibly Peter; Philip and potentially Nathaniel. In us, God sees more.

The Relational Potential for Salvation

Psychologists say we all have at least six friends. Every person has an existing group of people who form his or her network. A point of special note is that most of those who come to faith in Christ have dropped most of their non-Christian friends two years after conversion.[2] Therefore, Christians must be intentional about continually connecting with people outside the church. The most common title Jesus was given throughout his public ministry was "friend of sinners." It was not a term of endearment, at least not from the religious leaders who called Jesus such. But Jesus wore it as a badge of honor because he was constantly intentional about connecting with the not-yet-followers of God.

The potential for salvation through relationships can be demonstrated in the following visualization (see Figure 1). The starburst in the middle represents you, and the larger individual circles represent your interactions with others. With some of these people, we have superficial contact. With others, we connect more deeply and more often. We can use an acronym created by the United Methodist Church, FRAN, to indicate the difference in those relationships. F is for *Friends,* and R stands for *Relatives.* A stands for *Associates;* these are the people we know from work. N is for *Neighbors,* people in our network who are spiritually receptive. Each of these people is connected to another whole network, shown in Figure 1 by the smaller circles.

I never fail to be amazed at who I meet as I travel thousands of miles every year around this country. These encounters convince me of the truth of how proverbially small the world is. If this is true

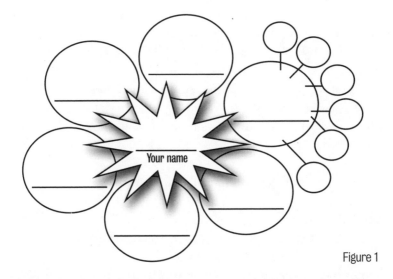

Figure 1

of our world today, I am sure it was true of the first-century world. The world at that time was populated with some 300 million people, about the same number as the population of the United States today.[3] Wherever he went, Paul must have greeted a friend's brother-in-law or a second cousin or aunt. Paul used his Christian connections to hook up with people who were not yet Christians.

The smallness of our world has been verified repeatedly. In 1967 Stanley Milgram published an article based on an experiment with chain letters to trace the average number of links between any two strangers in the United States, an experiment which became the source of the common expression "six degrees of separation." More recently, some sixty thousand people from 170 countries took part in a similar experiment. Of the hundreds of "chains" that have been completed, consistently the average number of links between any two human beings has been six.[4] This means that two total strangers will have an acquaintance or friend in common within just six relationships. The concept of six degrees of separation was applied by Karl Bunyan on the social networking site called Facebook.[5] The application calculates the degrees of separation in the relationships between different people. As of April 7, 2008, Facebook's website indicated it had about 4.5 million users. The average separation for all users of the application is 5.73 degrees (relationships), whereas the maximum degree of separation is 12.6. Consider your own network, be it online or face to face, personal or professional. All these relationships have the potential for spiritual impact.

Back to the Biblical Case Study

Let's finish out the story and this style. When Nathanael responds to Philip's invitation in John 1:46, he does so by asking if anything good could come from that northern rural community. Despite the geographic and cultural slur, Philip does not attempt to correct or convince him. He knows that is not his job. And neither is it ours, as I have said before. That is the work of the Holy Spirit. What Philip says to Nathanael is this: "Come and see" (v. 46). In other words, "I could stay here all day long and argue with you, but then it would be about me winning an argument and not about winning you to Jesus. So come and meet Jesus." Notice he does not *tell* Nathanael to go. Indicative of the relational component, Philip says, "Come. Let's do this together. You don't even have to believe what I'm saying at this point; just walk with me." This practice of sidling up to a non-Christian describes *belonging before believing*. It gives people a sense of connection with us, even if they do not yet have that connection with Christ.

As they approach, Jesus sees Nathanael and says to him, "Here is a true Israelite, in whom there is nothing false" (v. 47). Contemporarily speaking, Jesus was saying, "What you see is what you get. This is a true Israelite; he's faithful to his religious practices; he's a straight shooter; he tells you the way it is; he lays his cards on the table; he's not two-faced." Nathaniel asks Jesus, "How do you know me, seeing as we have never met before?" Jesus says, "Before

Philip approached you, I saw you sitting under the fig tree [culturally, a place of contemplation]. Not only are you a good guy, not only are you bright, not only are you moral, but you are also very religious, not just in your practices but in your thought processes." (I'm paraphrasing, of course.) The end of their conversation clearly shows Jesus had the ability to see people on the outside (sitting under a fig tree) as well as on the inside (Nathanael's personal integrity) (John 1:50-51).

But notice that even though Jesus affirmed his character and things were good, they were not good enough. If they were, Jesus would have left him alone. Rather, the Lord wanted Nathanael to keep coming in his direction. Why? Even with his virtues, there was still something not right. In Nathanael's case, it was prejudice. Look again at verse 48. Through the use of his divine power, Jesus sees Nathanael before Philip calls him. That also means Jesus most likely sees Nathanael when Philip calls him. Jesus hears the words that come out of Nathanael's mouth, words that are derogatory toward Nazareth in general and derogatory toward Jesus in particular. Coming to grips with what is wrong in his own life, his own sinfulness, Nathanael confesses his sin and acknowledges Jesus as Savior and Lord, and thereby makes a faith commitment. By contrast to the problems evident in Nathanael's life, "those coming to Christ today are beset with more past sins and problems and fewer moral standards than ever before."[6]

This passage affirms the power of just one person (Philip) to challenge and change another person (Nathanael). We do not find Philip the disciple saying any great theological thing like we hear from Peter, Philip the deacon, and Paul. They preached or spoke in a very structured manner or personal testimony. We do not find any of that taking place between Philip and Nathanael, because there was already a relationship, already an established rapport and respect. The reality was simple: "Come with me. We go here and there together, so why don't you come with me to meet Jesus?" All that occurred here was action—going somewhere, doing something together, not just talking. The importance of talking was diminished. What really took place there happened because of what had occurred over previous weeks, months, and years. Nathanael knew Philip was looking out for his best interests. So Nathanael gave Philip the benefit of any doubt. Nathanael doesn't fight Philip or argue with him, as would be the case between total strangers when one is not sure what the other person's real motivation or intention is. This happens because of the relationship already established.

Before I conclude, let me go back one more time to the importance of the relational style. Repeated studies through the years have shown that no less than 75 percent of people who have made a faith commitment to Christ did so because of the efforts and endeavors of people they knew, not the efforts of strangers.[7] Since the vast majority of early believers earned their living in purely secular ways, they spoke of their faith to those around them in this natural fashion.[8] The obvious conclusion is the vast majority of people made their faith commitment through the efforts of individuals other than clergy. According to a study of some 42,000 laypersons done by authors Win and Charles Arn, only 5-6 percent came to faith through the efforts of a pastor or member of the clergy.[9] By contrast, over 75 percent came to faith through the efforts of a friend or relative.[10] The principle is true: Faith is best shared by someone known, familiar and familial, not a stranger.

How does all this connect for those who come to Christ through a Graham-like crusade, a street preacher, or a door-to-door caller? The reality is those people will say that when they look over their spiritual shoulder, they see a line of people (the average is between nine and sixteen)[11] who tilled the soil, planted the seed, and nurtured the young plant of faith into fruition and fulfillment in the faith commitment that resulted from that final endeavor.

We cannot end without a word about when people reject the message about Jesus. Most rejection occurs because of the method of the messenger. In a study of 720 people, 84 percent stated that they said no thanks when the messenger acted like a teacher. When the messenger was perceived as a salesperson, 71 percent initially said yes but didn't stick with it. However, when the messenger was perceived as a friend, 94 percent said yes.[12] Relationships matter in sharing Jesus.

A survey of over 1000 people expressed these goals: 77 percent want to spend more time with family and friends; 73 percent want to save money; 61 percent want to make more money; 59 percent want to pursue personal hobbies and travel.[13] If we want to spend so much time with people we know, and we have so little time, it only makes sense that most of our evangelistic efforts will be with family and friends. Since each day is stubbornly 24 hours long, no more and no less, we have to work with the time we have and the people with whom we spend that time. We may have not thought about it before, but we need to realize that we have relational doors through which we can bring Jesus at any particular time. So I invite you to take a little time here and make a list of the people whom God used to bring you to faith in Christ.

_____   _____   _____

_____   _____   _____

Now make a list of the people who trace their commitment to Christ to a relationship with you.

_____   _____   _____

_____   _____   _____

God has no grandchildren. By faith we are daughters and sons of God. But we are the spiritual grandchildren of other believers who trusted Christ before us and shared their faith. We need to be the spiritual grandparents of those who will put their faith in Christ after us.

It has been documented that getting up in front of people is the number one fear in America. Fear of death is second. If you put those statistics together, you get a lot of people who are scared to death to speak in front of others! This reality could explain why the percentage of people with the assertive style of evangelism is so small. Our commitment to and relationship with people will avoid this near-death experience and will result in natural conversations about Christ, not confrontations for Christ. The real difference between word-based styles of evangelism and works-based styles of evangelism occurs here. As you get to know someone in a more personal way, you don't just keep repeating the same words over and over again. Time spent together allows you to find different things to talk about that lend themselves to new inroads for sharing the gospel in a conversational, relational manner.

Professor and author George Hunter III said, "Thirty years ago it probably took five 'significant encounters' before the average person would accept Christ as Savior. Today, because our culture is so disconnected from the gospel…the average convert to Christ will require between twelve and twenty 'significant touches' before they are saved."[14] Elmer Towns, cofounder of Liberty University, said it takes at least seven touches and three hearings of the gospel for a person to come to a point of decision to be a disciple.[15] From my own experiences and informal conclusions, people need about five connections with other believers in order to come to faith in Christ. Whatever the number, it is clear we are not to do evangelism alone. It is to be a shared responsibility among believers. I don't have to do it all alone, and I am not expected to do it all alone. Neither are you.

To understand this reality better, you are invited to make a list of minimum averages for each person you are trying to introduce to Jesus. Mention specifically what was done, when, and by whom.

One example is provided below.

Contacts (Touches)	Connections	Communications
1/14, I had lunch with John Steve who also likes to fish	2/21, I introduced John to Friend Sunday	3/29, I took John to Friend
_____	_____	_____
_____	_____	_____
_____	_____	_____

The point of the relational style is this: When we came to Christ, there was a celebration in heaven. But that celebration is ongoing inasmuch as God sees someone else who can come to Jesus through us, if we will share what someone else shared with us. A friend of mine said, "We have lots of people in our lives, but only a few folks." Granted, we all have lots of people we cross paths with, but when it comes to relational-style evangelism, we need to make the effort to evangelically invest ourselves in a few people. It is a matter of time and eternity.

NOTES
1. Mark Matteson with Kevin Thomas, *Customer Service Excellence* (Lynnwood, WA: Pinnacle Service Group, Inc., 2005), 33.
2. R. Larry Moyer, *31 Days with the Master Fisherman* (Grand Rapids: Kregel Publications, 1997), 44.
3. Murray Bourne, *Interactive Mathematics,* http://www.intmath.com/Exponential-logarithmic-functions/world-population-live.php (accessed March 18, 2009).
4. Thomas Berman, "Six Degrees of Separation: Fact or Fiction?" *Primetime,* ABC News, December 12, 2006.

5. Karl Bunyan, "Microsoft's Six Degrees of Separation Experiment," *K!*, August 4, 2008. http://www.karlbunyan.co.uk/2008/08/microsofts-six-degrees-of-separation.aspx (accessed March 19, 2009). See also David Smith, "Proof! Just Six Degrees of Separation Between Us," *The Observer*, August 3, 2008. http://www.guardian.co.uk/technology/2008/aug/03/internet.email (accessed March 19, 2009).

6. Moyer, 60.

7. These studies can be found in the following works: Lyle E. Schaller, "Six Targets for Growth," *The Lutheran*, September 3, 1975; Win Arn and Charles Arn, *The Master's Plan for Making Disciples* (Pasadena: Church Growth Press, 1982), 43; "We're Glad You Asked," *Jews for Jesus Newsletter* 6 (5744/1984): 4; Ron Crandall, *The Contagious Witness* (Nashville: Abingdon Press, 1999), 70; Steve Sjogren and Dave Ping, *Outflow* (Colorado Springs: Group Publishing, 2007), 139.

8. Kenneth Scott Latourette, *A History of the Expansion of Christianity* (New York: Harper Publishing, 1939), 1: 116, quoted in.

9. Arn and Arn, 46.

10. Ibid., 46. Michael Green puts the number at 77 percent in *Sharing Your Faith with Friends and Family* (Grand Rapids: Baker Books, 2005), 11.

11. William Carr Peel and Walt Larimore, *Going Public with Your Faith* (Grand Rapids: Zondervan, 2003), 107.

12. Flavil Yeakley, "Research and the Growing Church," *Church Growth America*, January-February 1981, 10, quoted in Arn, 100.

13. Alton Cumberbatch, "The Personal Need," *SMI: Succes Motivation International, Inc.* http://www.success-motivation.com/fl/whysmi.php (accessed May 1, 2009).

14. From a conversation between Steve Sjogren and George Hunter III, as quoted by James A. Simpson, *Unbind Him, Lazarus 4* (sermon, Christ United Methodist Church, Independence, MO, March 25, 2007) http://icumc.org/sermonlazarus4.pdf (accessed May 1, 2009).

15. Elmer Towns as quoted by Larry Gilbert, *Team Evangelism: How to Influence Your Loved Ones for Christ* (Lynchburg, VA; Church Growth Institute, 1991), 103.

CHAPTER 6

the invitational style,
or "would you like to come?"

If you return to the styles chart on page 11, you will note that the invitational style of evangelism is sandwiched in between the relational style on the left and the incarnational style on the right. This is no accident. Since relational-style evangelism focuses on people, and incarnational-style evangelism focuses on projects, invitational-style evangelism combines some of each. The evangelizer seeks out the evangelized to do something (incarnational) together (relational). The process by which these two styles get together describes the invitational style.

As previously said, each of the three works-based styles has a different orientation. The relational style is people oriented. The invitational style is event oriented, focusing on shared experiences. The events can be small or large activities, like going to a seasonal event in a home, a sports event, concert, craft fair, or an antique car show. The point is that the evangelizer and the evangelized attend the event together. In all these three remaining styles, there is an emphasis on being alongside one another, doing something together. Even though the emphasis here is on action-based events, this style could not exist without the presence of the other styles, especially the storytelling style, because so many events—plays, concerts, and movies, for instance—are word-based.

Invitational people are hospitable people. They are inclusive. They are constantly thinking about others. They do not even go to the store without thinking about someone else going along or at least calling someone to ask if they could pick up something for him or her. They automatically think of others when reading, hearing, or seeing anything. These are the people you want to have buying you presents! They know their friends' sizes and preferences—often keeping a mental record of friends' likes and interests—and therefore, they always select that perfect gift. In a word, they have generous spirit toward others.

My wife is one of these people. She thinks of others early and often. She sees something for someone in February that would be just perfect as a Christmas gift. But then in May she finds something that is even better—and in August finds something even better than that. Before Christmas we have multiple gifts bought for people. When I ask in November which one of those gifts we are going to give to a particular person for Christmas, she says, "All of them." The recipient of the invitational-style person either does really well with the holidays, or those gifts just keep on getting pushed back to be given on another occasion. By contrast, assertive-style people are not the ones you want buying you gifts. They buy you what they think you need. Their gifts tend to have a subliminal message about something they want you to do or want you to change. At the least, they tend to buy you something they would like to have themselves, because they believe that what they want or need, everyone else should, too.

In many years and miles of travel and attendance at more church suppers and public functions than I can recount, I have learned that women seem to be intrinsically better than men at the invitational style. I have been seated at many a table and watched a woman rise and say to the group, "I need to use the restroom. Would any of you ladies like to come along?" Sure enough, without hesitation, at least one accepts the invitation. It's no wonder, then, that one poll has found that "event-based evangelism was more likely to be used by women than men."[1] Women demonstrate a natural tendency to be invitational and group oriented, which is the heart and soul of the invitational style.

Pros and Cons of the Invitational Style

In the other chapters, I have made reference to the negative and positive aspects of each personality style. We have already highlighted the invitational personality's strength is hospitality—a natural and inclusive desire to welcome someone into an experience. The negative quality that is closely related to this strength, however, is the tendency to mistake someone's presence for someone's acceptance. It's all too easy for invitational personalities to think that their evangelistic responsibility is fulfilled by inviting and accompanying a guest or friend to a Christian-based event. But there is more to accepting Jesus than accepting an invitation to the latest concert, revival, Bible study, or Christian fellowship.

Where the word-based styles on the left may say too much, these styles on the right may say too little. People think, no matter how subconsciously, that others will get the spiritual message by osmosis. That is the inherent spiritual danger. In the invitational style more than other works-based styles, evangelizers often depend on someone else to do the talking instead of the evangelizers talking themselves. There still needs to be a moment when the evangelizer says something to the evangelized, even if it is in the privacy of the car while traveling to or from an event. The evangelizer's words reinforce and make personal whatever spiritual message is publicly given.

The Invitational Style in Action

Occupations that suit the invitational style person are hosts or hostesses; event planners; or program directors on cruise ships, in activities centers, or at camps. They believe an experience is enhanced when it is shared. If they had a life motto, it would be "the more, the merrier."

The invitational style is extremely important if you are interested in reaching the postmodern culture. Think about it. Young people travel in herds. You would be hard-pressed to go to the mall on any Friday or Saturday evening and see a teenager walking alone. They look for places to go and things to do together. Their nature as adolescents is by default relational. In teens, we see the free flow between the styles because the relational and invitational styles complement the storytelling style, especially in the aspect of music. Think of the large number of teenagers who attend concerts. They are the largest segment of our society who buys music, online and in stores.[2]

The Potential of the Invitational Style

Think for a moment now what would happen if we intentionally did a very small piece of what teens do naturally. If we used the invitational style more fully, every church—regardless of its location—could literally double its attendance without adding one parking space. Everyone who comes to church just needs to bring someone else, and I do not mean another person who is already a church member. I am talking about bringing someone who is new to the Christian church. One study points out that only 2 percent of church people invite an unchurched person.[3] No church has more people inside it on a Sunday morning than the number of people who live in the community or surrounding area. During the hour of the worship service, most congregations have more people drive by their church buildings than are present inside. And many of those people who pass by may not even notice that the churches are there.

For this invitational style to work, we need to get to know some people who are not in the church whom we can invite. Here again, I am talking about the invitational *come,* not the commanding *go.* People may be reluctant to go to church by themselves, but they may welcome an invitation to go with someone else. Noted church researcher and founder of the Barna Group, George Barna has observed that 21 percent of unchurched people would come to church if asked,[4] while Rainer's research says more than 80 percent would come if asked.[5] There is no clear explanation for the disparity between those numbers; if we let the figures form the low and high parameters, the truth most likely lies somewhere in between. This much we know: Nearly two-thirds of people remain unasked, and two-thirds of Christians are not asking. If our church is good enough for us, it ought to be good enough for someone else. (If you don't feel comfortable inviting someone to your church, perhaps you need to look for a new church!)

The invitational style also piggybacks on the "coming along side me" idea, which we just saw in the relational style. In other words, you and I don't have to believe the same thing to go to a function that we both might enjoy. Invitational-style evangelizers look for high-quality events to take their friends to.

Andrew, Master of Invitations
If we look in the Bible for an example of the invitational style, Andrew comes to mind (John 1:35-42). He is first presented as a disciple of John the baptizer. In this passage, Jesus has come and has been baptized by John, who served as the announcer of Jesus' public ministry. Andrew then, with unnamed others, approaches Jesus and asks him this question: "Where are you living?" (v. 38). Jesus' answer is "come and see" (v. 39). Here we witness a process in which Jesus allows these seekers to belong or hang around before they believe, prior to becoming disciples. Jesus does not ask them to make a decision on the spot. He just asks them to walk with him, see where he lives, get to know him, and see where things might go from there. Then Andrew, having spent the entire day hanging out with Jesus, goes and shares that news—not with a total stranger, not with someone he does not know—but instead his elder brother, Peter, someone with whom he has had a lifelong relationship and rapport. Later, Philip does the same thing.

In more recent times, we see the impact of the invitational style in the fact that 80 percent of those who attended Billy Graham crusades came because of an invitation made through a relational connection.[6] Investing leads to inviting. When we are intentional about spending time with others, whether they are family members or friends, in most cases they will in turn want to spend time with us and be interested in what interests us.

We have to stop here and talk about an historical anomaly of human relationships. The first of the four Gospels to be written was the Gospel of Mark. It is included in the canon of Scripture because it received historical and apostolic approval from none other than the apostle Peter. Although Peter did not write the Gospel himself, his personally shared information about the ministry of Jesus was the basis for the book. He approved it as Mark penned it. This fact was affirmed by Irenaeus in the second century, as well as by others before and after him in the early church. The Gospel of Mark mentions Andrew only in a list of the twelve disciples (as do the Gospels of Matthew and Luke). But if we compare Mark's account with the Gospel of John, we find in John that Peter came to Jesus through Andrew's invitation. The Gospel of Mark does not give any indication of this. I have always found that quite intriguing. Why did Peter not instruct Mark to explain that Andrew was the first disciple? I believe there is an appropriate explanation. It seems that toward the end of the first century, the author of the Gospel of John came along and, under the inspiration of the Holy Spirit, told us the rest of the story. It looks like the author was saying, "I need to let you all in on something, something that obviously has not been shared with everybody. Even though Peter was a person of prominence and influence throughout this first century, Peter was not the first disciple of Jesus. Andrew was. Peter came to faith in Christ because of the evangelistic efforts and witness of Andrew."

Why is it important for us to notice that the Gospel of Mark does not indicate Andrew was the first disciple? I believe it makes a significant point about evangelism, one that ties everything together and connects this with the rest of the evangelism styles. Peter and his assertive personality did not necessarily want people to remember that he was not the first disciple. Aren't you glad God works with us as we are? Here we see the humanity of a person coming out in the holy pages of the Bible. Peter's omission can be explained through the dynamics of sibling relationships. God allowed his character to be transparent and evident, even in sacred script. As the elder brother, he was probably the one who ran the family, as he seems to have run everything and everybody (or at least tried to!). Peter did not want the world to remember that he, Peter, was not the first to come to Christ. Let's face it. If Peter were your older brother, you might not have talked for yourself until you were in your teens!

I cannot emphasize enough how an earthly relationship can be used by the Holy Spirit to lead to a heavenly one, especially those within the context of family. One study found 37 percent of Christians linked their conversion to being invited to church.[7] Clearly, over one third of all professing Christians say they experienced their conversion within the walls of a church building and got there only because someone else had invited them to attend with them. The power of the invitation and what can come from it cannot be denied.

So, in the very first chapter of the Fourth Gospel, the writer establishes that Andrew was the first disciple, not Peter, as many early believers might have assumed. Subsequently, every time Andrew is mentioned, he is introducing someone to Jesus. He introduces his brother Peter to Jesus (John 1). Andrew introduces the lad with the lunch to Jesus (John 6). Andrew introduces the Greeks with questions to Jesus (John 12). Younger or older people, individuals or groups, Andrew—complementary to his more passive personality—was always introducing someone to Jesus. The simplistic and practical definition of biblical evangelism is inviting someone to meet Jesus. Introducing someone to Jesus might be an even better definition. If we make the definition of evangelism any more than inviting people to meet Jesus, we create loopholes we can slip though and thereby absolve ourselves intellectually of any individual participation and responsibility. Andrew becomes a clear and simple example for us of the invitational style.

In Andrew, we also see the multiculturalism that continues to come to life in Scripture. Whether they were people he knew or were strangers, people he was related to or were foreigners, Andrew demonstrated evangelism by simply introducing all these different kinds of people to Jesus. At sometime in our lives, every one of us has performed an introduction, be if of ourselves or of someone else. We all can and all do this. Those who are better at this than others are more than likely wired in this invitational way. When it comes to evangelism, invitational-style people simply bring people to Jesus, make the necessary introductions, and then leave the rest of the relationship-building to the Lord.

Individual Expression and Corporate Expression
Consider this pair of statistics. Barna's research says a few will come into our churches if asked—one out of every four;[8] however, Rainer's research says more than three out of five would come to our *homes* if asked.[9] If you think about the invitational style, you begin to see that it has two substyles. One substyle is the individual expression; the other is the corporate expression. One is a home-based invitational, evangelistic experience and the other is church-based. An example of the home-based, individual substyle happens when Andrew goes where Jesus is dwelling prior to the beginning of his public ministry. Andrew asks Jesus, "Where do you live?" Jesus invites him to come and see. The passage says that they spent the day together (John 1:39). So, before Andrew ever makes a decision to truly follow Jesus, he first wants to get to know Jesus—not in a synagogue or the temple, but in his residence, where the "real" Jesus lives.

A generation or two ago, the home-based substyle of invitational evangelism could be an organic part of community life. Fifty or sixty years ago, people would never have thought of constructing a home without a front porch. That was a family's place for connecting with the world. Neighbors would call to one another and children would congregate there on rainy days. Today, most new homes are constructed with stoops, many without even an eave overhead. We are more likely to congregate only with immediate family in the privacy of a fenced yard or a private deck, accessible only through the house. We are selective about who we let into these private places, the sacred spaces of our lives.

Today, we must be more intentional about nurturing home-based invitational opportunities. It invites (and demands) a more intimate level of hospitality. Such opportunities might include Bible studies in your living room or Vacation Bible School in your front yard; they might also involve fellowship over a family barbeque or a simple invitation to join you for coffee, tea, and dessert. Never underestimate the bonding power of a home-cooked meal! Many of the Gospel stories feature food prominently, whether Jesus was multiplying loaves and fishes or teaching over a meal with tax collectors or serving his disciples the first Lord's Supper. The table is a great space for nourishing relationships as well as bodies, for cultivating conversations that build trust and facilitate transitions from the mundane to the divine.

With a return to a residence-based, small-group model of ministry in some congregations, evangelism that begins in a home serves to identify that home as a Christian one, as well as to build connections with people in that community on their terms and turf. It truly allows for the gospel to be shared in a natural and neighborly way.

When it comes to the church-based substyle of invitation, there is a lot of discussion about services or events geared just toward "seekers" versus those designed for "saints." But as I read the Scriptures, there seems to be an expectation that both kinds of people will be in attendance together. The apostle Paul lays out specific guidelines as to the exercise of the visual and verbal gifts, so that all things are done decently and in order, preventing offense or confusion for those who do not yet believe (1 Corinthians 14). Obviously, these early believers worshipped in private homes where people came and went constantly. There was a continual interaction between those in and outside the Christian faith. What was true then is still necessary today. So, in planning church-based invitational events, we need to consider the needs of both seeker and seasoned saint. Be sure that your event hosts are helpful to visitors, and aim for a program that offers solid gospel content without churchy jargon. And keep in mind that even saints enjoy an event that offers pure clean fun and opportunity for fellowship! The relationships that are borne out of such entertainments can become the foundation for later conversations about weightier things.

To bridge the gap between home-based invitations and invitations at the church level, my local church regularly does two different kinds of invitational outreach. Our Fall Festival provides for nonthreatening interaction between Christians and non-Christians, centered around food and fun, and open to the community. I believe that if we get people inside the church for something not directly related to "church," those people might show up on Sunday morning, because now they are more familiar with the building and have met some people. We also have a regular evangelistic service we call Invite-a-Friend Sunday, usually the last Sunday morning of each month. The suggestion is that we make friends with people who are not members of our congregation or believers in Christ and invite them to a service that is specifically geared in content to their lack of familiarity with the church. During those services, a clear presentation of the gospel is made. Our minister of music uses familiar old hymns during the service, but the songs have more contemporary melodies. Author and pastor

Randy Recton says this type of ministry can be done about four times a year with good results.[10] I have found it can be done twice as often, especially if your church has people strong in the invitational style.

Pastor and author Derek Prime believes an appeal for a faith commitment can be extended in several different ways other than the traditional invitation to come forward at the conclusion of the service.[11] You can offer people the opportunity to meet with the speaker or another appointed individual after the service in a designated place. This meeting can either be for individual sharing or for a group experience so as not to single anyone out. Another possibility is to simply give booklets or DVDs containing a gospel presentation to those who ask for them when the service is over. Still another option is to provide response cards in the bulletin. These cards can then be handed to the speaker or placed in a basket in the vestibule on the way out of church for later follow-up at a mutually convenient time and private place. You can even invite people to make a commitment right where they are sitting in the sanctuary, eliminating the need to move from their seats or to come down the aisle. I encourage you to allow people to make their faith commitment through a prayer in their own words, not the words of others. Doing so seems to cement the decision and helps a person to own the new relationship with God.

As you can see with the invitational style, actions are primary. I could give you pages and pages of examples. Instead, I invite you to spend the time it would take to read those pages and put this book aside. Pick up the phone and call a friend or relative. Say hi and find out how she is doing. Go across the street to your neighbor's home and knock on the door. Invite him to dinner on Friday or to church Sunday. Regardless of whether your invitation is to home- or church-based location, the door that is the most welcoming is the door of personal invitation.[12] So we must become personally involved with people to make that kind of invitation.

NOTES

1. George Barna, "Survey Shows How Christians Share Their Faith" *The Barna Group,* January 31, 2005, http://www.barna.org/barna-update/article/5-barna-update/186-survey-shows-how-christians-share-their-faith (accessed May 1, 2009).

2. See "Putting Christ in Mainstream Media" http://www.kingdomgrant.org/archangel/mediapg4htm (accessed May 27, 2009).

3. Thom Rainer, *The Unchurched Next Door* (Grand Rapids: Zondervan, 2003), 25.

4. George Barna, *The State of the Church, 2000* (Ventura, CA: Barna Research Group, 2000), 1. www.barna.org

5. Rainer, 24.

6. Lon Allison and Mark Anderson, *Going Public with the Gospel: Reviving Evangelistic Proclamation* (Downers Grove, IL: InterVarsity Press, 2004), 78, 159.

7. Derek Prime, *Active Evangelism* (Fearn, Tain, Ross-shire, Scotland, UK: Christian Focus Publications, 2003), 22.

8. Barna, *The State of the Church, 2000.*

9. Rainer, 202.

10. Randy Becton, *Everyday Evangelism* (Grand Rapids: Baker Books, 1997), 84.

11. Prime, 105–06.

12. David McIntyre quoted by Tom Clegg and Warren Bird, *Lost in America* (Colorado Springs: Group Publishing, 2001), 24. McIntyre is senior pastor, Calvary Evangelical Free Church in Trumbull, Connecticut.

CHAPTER 7

the incarnational style,

or "preach the gospel at all times; when necessary use words"

In this chapter, we will explore the last of the six personality-based evangelism styles in this book. This style is dubbed the incarnational style of evangelism, and like several of the other styles, has two sub-styles, which we will examine later. The incarnational style takes its meaning from the word *incarnate*, which Dictionary.com defines as "embodied in flesh." The incarnational style is the final of the three styles and grows out of the works-based category of evangelism—sharing the gospel in a tangible way. As we come to this final style, one important fact needs to be noted. Though one specific style—the relational style of evangelism—deals specifically with relational matters, *all* styles need to be relational to some degree if they are to be effective. In the first style we examined, the assertive style, those relationships will be more superficial than in any other. However, even with the assertive style, there still must be some intentionality in creating some kind of connection. Lon Allison confirms this by noting that 83 percent of those who made decisions at a crusade (public assertive methodology), subsequently became members of churches where they already had an existing relationship with a friend or family member.[1] It is clear that relationships are significant in the successful long-term results for the assertive style.

So by the time we come to the incarnational style of evangelism, the relational component is at its maximum. It is where our witness takes on the sense of "with-ness," and we see the balance between life and lips. This style involves linking up with people and walking alongside them—not for minutes, not for hours, not for days or even weeks—but months that literally spill over into years. You cannot help but have that magnitude and depth of involvement with someone else when there is a clear relational component.

Before we examine the incarnational style in detail, let's draw an important link among all the styles. Looking again at the styles chart on page 11, we have been viewing it and referring to it in a linear fashion, as printed on the flat page. Now I would ask you to see it instead as cylindrical and three-dimensional. (See Figure 1.) If you do this, what you see happening is that it all comes around, as pretty much everything in life does. On the far left side of the chart (assertive) as well as on the far right side of the chart (incarnational), we have what we could describe as personality extremes. The assertive style is extreme in its verbal presentation of the gospel, and the incarnational style is extreme in its vocational presentation of the gospel. In reality, both those styles share at least one aspect in common: intense passion. The other styles may demonstrate purpose, but probably none of the others demonstrates passion to the degree that these two extremes do. I guess, in part, that is what makes them extremes.

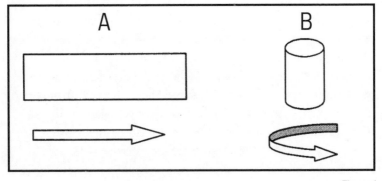

Figure 1

As I have noted in the last two chapters, each of the three styles under the broad works-based category has a distinct and different orientation. Relational-style evangelism is people oriented, and invitational style evangelism is event oriented. Incarnational-style evangelism is needs oriented. More than any other style, the incarnational style sees and pays attention to human need. It sees a problem, short- or long-term, and does something tangible about it. This is the style that most fully combines an awareness of both the temporal and the eternal.

Pros and Cons of the Incarnational Style

Compassionate and needs-oriented, incarnational people enjoy helping others in tangible, practical ways, rather than getting into long philosophical discussions they often perceive as irrelevant. These people would rather work with their hands than their heads. They prefer to express Christian love through actions rather than words. Incarnational people believe actions will help others to listen to what they have to say about Christ. These are empathetic people, not just sympathetic individuals. *Sympathy* is when one person feels the emotions of someone else. *Empathy* goes further. It is the ability to imagine oneself in another person's situation. But empathy is more than a feeling; it motivates and moves a person to do something about another person's difficult circumstances.

Empathy is a key component in the makeup of the incarnational personality, and as such it is both a strength and a potential weakness. Incarnational personalities are often employed in human service professions, such as health care or social work. They may also excel in pastoral counseling or chaplaincy ministries. In all such vocations, they are inevitably susceptible to burnout. They take on too much of their clients' pain, and as a result, the servant is too vulnerable and weakened to serve.

There is another component to the incarnational personality. These people are industrious and in some form or another would be considered handy. More than any of the other styles, the incarnational-style person knows how to get things done. These are the people who find great joy in participating in Meals on Wheels programs, Habitat for Humanity work, or in food pantries and clothing closets. They are the doers in life, those who take seriously the words attributed to Francis of Assisi: "Preach the gospel always, and when necessary use words."

The incarnational personality style's preference for actions over words can be a weakness when it comes to leading people to Jesus. After all, Jesus was the Word incarnate, and even he occasionally needed words to interpret his actions for the crowds and his own disciples.

The Incarnational Style in Action

Specific examples of occupations that fall within the incarnational style are many, but I will lift up just one: nurses. I single out nurses because what they do goes beyond the relational aspect of life. If they were simply relational, caring, and people oriented, one patient—especially a child—would be their undoing. Confronted by a patient's suffering due to an extreme illness would be more than enough for them to just chuck it all, resign, and head on home. But day after day after day, these people return to the same hospital wards and continue to minister to the people in the same beds, although those people may be different day by day. Nurses do not connect so much with a specific person as much as they connect with a problem. Their belief—and rightly so—is that they can make a difference. Their conviction is that their efforts matter. That they are making a difference keeps them coming back, day after day.

When we connect this personality with evangelism, we encounter a style of evangelism that is as old as the Christian church. In the earliest records of the church, believers "sold property and posses-sions to give to *anyone* who had need" (Acts 2:45, italics added). These believers saw a need and did what was necessary to meet it, regardless of whether or not the person in need was a Christian. This pattern of evangelism has continued throughout the church's history. Many social reforms have had their birth in the church; when disaster strikes, believers—individually and corporately—are among the first to respond.

An excellent biblical example of the incarnational style is Dorcas in Acts 9. The story of Dorcas emphasizes the action-to-address-need aspect of this style. In this passage, we are hard-pressed to find anywhere that Dorcas verbally says anything to share the Good News. Undoubtedly she did, but Dorcas's primary witness is what she has in her hand, not in her mouth. God affirmed such. So great was her witness that when she died, God sent two of the highest-ranking church officials from her town to get Peter, who raised her back to life. That tells us one of two things, perhaps both. Dorcas's testimony was so great that God said, in effect, "The world cannot do without this sister's labor for me. Let's bring her back to life, put her up on her feet again, and get her going for my mission." It may also tell us that the Lord said, "You know what? It is easier to raise Dorcas back to life than to get ten other church members to do her job!" Either way, it appears that God highly values those who put their witnesses into tangible, concrete action.

Let me remind you of something else we find in the witness of Dor-cas. Life ought to back up lips. The walk should support the talk. But, there needs to be a balance between what we do and what we say. "Others are watching you live your life; you need to watch the life you live."[2] The incarnational style is about doing the message be-fore (as well as concurrently with) telling the message with your lips. We all instinctively know that "walking the talk" is absolutely nec-essary. We all know of an example where someone's actions either strengthened or undermined the effectiveness of his or her words.

The Substyles: Service and Servant Incarnational Evangelism

There are two substyles under incarnational evangelism. The first is what I refer to as service incarnational evangelism;[3] the second is servant incarnational evangelism. Let me explain the differences.

Service Incarnational Evangelism

Service evangelism involves short-term engagement. These actions are intentional but sporadic acts of kindness: doing one good thing. The purpose of service evangelism is to get the church outside its walls and to raise awareness of the church's presence in the community.

I remember going into a small town to speak. Though I had directions to the town, I did not have them to the church. I figured once I arrived in the community, I would get directions. I did just that, pulling up to the first convenience store I saw. I asked the rather sleepy-looking cashier on that early Sunday morning where First Baptist Church was located. She shook her head and said, "I have lived in this town all my life and didn't know there was a First Baptist." I thanked her for her time and decided to head out and see if I could find it on my own. I did. It really wasn't difficult to locate; it was just two blocks away from the convenience store where I had just stopped! I began my message that morning with this introduction: "Do you folks know that if First Baptist closed tomorrow, the cashier at the convenience store down the street could not care less? And I have to wonder how many other people she represents in this community." No doubt that was not the gentlest of sermon beginnings, but the reality I shared was a wake-up call for that congregation. This congregation's experience raises a similar question for your congregation: If your church closed tomorrow, how many people in your community would notice or care?

Another characteristic of service incarnational evangelism is that its absence probably will not cause long-term hurt or deprivation. For example, it is a hot day in the summer. Your congregation packs up several coolers with popsicles and cold bottles of water and heads to a local park. You pass out these items to parents and their kids. These folks are refreshed and grateful. If you did not do it, no one would really be any worse off. Demonstrating that you thought about those people and did something nice for them raised the awareness of your church's presence in that community.

The point of service incarnational evangelism is to begin to address our apparent invisibility and irrelevance. It helps us make initial contact in a non-threatening way for both parties (evangelizer and evangelized), allowing believers to begin to see the needs of others and to start to address them over time. So many of our churches have been closed up and closed off from our communities that we are not able to honestly engage people short- or long-term, because we have no integrity with them. Service evangelism, short-term, gets the church outside its walls and creates the possibilities for long-term engagement.

Back to the story of the "invisible" church I shared above. That Sunday afternoon over a consultation luncheon, I was asked by one of the leaders what the church should do to address the community's lack of awareness of their presence. Since it was autumn, I fell back on a standard service project. "Pass out batteries for people's smoke detectors," I said, and explained the simple concept. That was that. Almost two years later, I crossed paths with the church's pastor. He asked me if I remembered him, and I had to confess that I did not. He said, "I am pastor of the church you told to pass out batteries a year and a half ago." "Oh, yes, how did that go?" I asked. He said that in their small community, they passed out two thousand nine-volt batteries. I stood there stunned. They were not a big church. At a conservative cost of two dollars each, that is four thousand dollars for just one outreach. When I asked how they paid for it, the pastor said they went to the chamber of commerce, the town council, the Red Cross, the Rotarians, and other civic and social groups and received numerous donations. I asked what became of their efforts. He said no one came into the church from their canvassing. But, everywhere he went, he was known as *the battery pastor,* and his people were known as *the battery church.* I said, "Not too bad. Two years ago, you were known for nothing. Today, they call you *the battery church.* Two years from now, you could be the center of the community's spiritual health and vitality, where people come not to get their batteries changed, but to get their lives changed." Being known for acts of kindness is better than not being known at all. But I also reminded him that a church's primary role in every community is introducing people to Christ. If incarnational acts are only acts by us, for us, then they will not lead to the acts of the Holy Spirit done through us. Service evangelism raises our integrity with our neighbors because it conveys that they matter. It brings the church to them, instead of the common perception that they have to come to us.

A church in Kentucky did door-to-door calling to raise awareness of their new church plant in the community. They passed out energy-efficient light bulbs as a way to do something good for the environment, as well as to let folks try them before investing in them. In just over three hours (averaging less than two minutes per encounter), twenty-one families distributed light bulbs to over two thousand homes. Clearly, the purpose was to get the church people out into the community and to raise the community's awareness of that church. The response to their efforts was better than average. The first weekend after the canvassing, eleven people came to worship; eventually seventeen families started to attend.[4] However, that worked out to less than one tenth of one percent of all the people they came in contact with. Steve Sjogren says that typically six months will pass before the full fruit of this substyle of evangelism appears in the local church. It is best to wait a year before looking at the numbers of new people coming to the church as a result of these activities.[5] These figures are based on at least a monthly engagement with the community to maintain the awareness. From my experience, I would concur. Service evangelism is not going to change your church or community overnight. It is not supposed to. Service incarnational-style evangelism is meant to change the church and the way it interacts with its community. It is the first step for churches that have not connected with their communities, before they move into the more involved commitments required in servant evangelism.

Servant Incarnational Evangelism

The second substyle is servant incarnational evangelism. It is the epitome of the works-sharing style of our faith. In service evangelism, you show up, do your thing, and head home within an hour or two. You cannot do that with the kind of needs addressed by servant-style evangelism. These needs are deep and long-term human needs like abuse (all types), homelessness, hunger, mental illness, education, literacy, family issues, and delinquency. Servant-style evangelism describes the efforts of God's people to make a needed change in society, in both individuals and institutions, to alleviate conditions that hurt people and diminish their divine value. Being creations of Almighty God, people bear God's stamp of manufacturing. As followers of Christ, we have the responsibility to improve an individual's lot in life in whatever way we can and to address these societal problems, even if people do not make commitments to follow Christ. It is what Jesus would have done. *It is what Jesus did.* It is what Jesus wants to do *through* us. More than any other style, servant incarnational evangelism demonstrates that by validating a person's inherent worth, that individual might become open to the inspired Word. When we touch the outside of someone, we also potentially touch the inside of someone.

E. Stanley Jones, noted evangelist and missionary to India throughout the better part of the 1900s, addressed the inherent pitfall in the extremes of these passions—to transform both the inside and outside of a person. "The social gospel [incarnational-style evangelism], divorced from personal salvation, is like a body without a soul; the message of personal salvation [assertive-style evangelism], without a social dimension, is like a soul without a body. The former is a corpse; the latter is a ghost."[6] Therefore, the incarnational style understands more and better than any other style that we must minister to *both parts,* regardless of any personal decision made for Jesus Christ. The ministry is done unconditionally as an example of God's grace, regardless of the recipient's response. Although we are not the originators of God's grace, we are its facilitators. The Bible calls us *administrators, dispensers,* or *stewards* of grace (1 Peter 4:10). Grace does not begin with us, but it can be stopped by us, like turning a faucet on and off. The church is called to minister redemptively. People will often experience the love of God for the first time through incarnational evangelism but not even recognize the significance of what has happened. Sometimes the one doing the deed is as unaware of the significance as the one who receives it. For both, it is like the proverbial cup of cold water to a parched soul.

In the relational style chapter, I spoke to one reality of how you can minister to postmodern people and get them on board in the work of the church. The incarnational style speaks to their experience. They are looking for ways to make tangible differences in their communities, whether they are Christians or not. Christians and non-Christians often work beside each another on a Habitat for Humanity house. Why can't a Christian share a testimony while sharing tools? A natural way to get the conversation going would be for the Christian to ask the other person why he or she is spending a Saturday building a house for someone else. The social gospel Jones advocated in the early 1900s emphasized doing good works *and* being sure to share the Good News. Servant evangelism best lives out this principle of true biblical justice.

The Incarnational Style: Risks and Benefits

When we deal with incarnational-style evangelism, we come face-to-face with our motivations for evangelism. Consciously or unconsciously, we often "do evangelism" so others will help us keep our church going. We end up viewing the evangelized (the lost) as a means (to our church's survival) and not as an end in and of themselves. However, the people our churches are called to reach may not be able to offer anything tangible to our congregations. Still, what they have to give is meaningful. It is not and should not be for monetary reasons that we do what we do for them. We do not reach out to people to get more people in the pews and more money in the plates. *We reach out to people because Christ commanded it.* This is not—nor should it ever be—about nickels or noses. This is about letting people in their unbelieving state come inside the church as we build relationships with them. We do this so they can experience a sense of belonging to the church family, even before they experience the salvation that actually brings them into the family of God.

In contrast with service evangelism, with its intentional but sporadic acts of kindness—a type of quick "spiritual come-and-go"—servant incarnational-style evangelism has a much more systematic approach and impact. It involves doing community canvassing and looking at the demographics of a church's context. It targets certain issues, taking the words of Jesus literally: "the poor you will always have with you" (Mark 14:7). The word *poor* means people who lack something needed for basic human survival. People can be poor vocationally, physically, emotionally, as well as spiritually. Moving from *service* evangelism to *servant* evangelism requires a huge leap in time and energy from a congregation.

Servant evangelism fully understands that we cannot do everything, but it recognizes that we can do *something*. It leads us to put in place a systematic strategy to target issues and make inroads into people's lives and problems. It is important here to distinguish between people and their problems. The two are *not* the same. Servant evangelism raises awareness of needs in the community, regardless of how uncomfortable some people, who would rather deny the ill exists, may feel. The church advocates for struggling people and says as a body of people, "We're not satisfied with the status quo." Servant evangelism acknowledges the presence of the problem and accepts responsibility to solve it. The church also recognizes the importance of partnering with community-based organizations, Christian or not, to address these matters. Our cooperation and collaboration demonstrate that believers are not just concerned about the hereafter of people's lives, but also the here and now. Let's face it. It is hard to think about a home in heaven tomorrow, when you don't have a home here on earth to call your own today.

In summary, here is a simplistic chart showing the distinctives and differences of each of the substyles under the incarnational style (see page 11).

Service Evangelism	Servant Evangelism
Short-term engagement	Long(er)-term engagement
Get the church outside the walls	Get the church inside people's lives
Intentional, but arbitrarily selected acts	Systematic, project-oriented approach
Raise awareness of the church in the community	Raise awareness of the need in the community
Focus on the messenger	Focus on the (gospel) message

I spoke to this earlier, but I want to raise it again: Rejection is a real possibility, even when doing good. Rejection, or the fear of it, is one reason why most Christians do not do evangelism. But it is paramount that we do not take rejection personally. Similar to personal assertive evangelism, service evangelism does not put us in contact with people for very long. They may not like what we do, but they do not have issues with us personally. This is true especially if what we are offering them is something like a bottle of water, a battery for a smoke detector, or a coupon for a free pizza. In servant evangelism, on the other hand, the rejection is muted because the amount of time we spend with other people serves to cancel out any suspicion. We often reject what we do not know. The long-term benefits of servant evangelism make the church outward-focused and moves the congregation toward action. The church will be refocused by and in its surrounding community. The church will be alive in doing deeds with spiritual impact and will itself become redefined through its actions. This style of evangelism is meant to create an audience with non-Christians in a nonthreatening manner, both for the givers and the recipients. Whether a church offers short-term, intentional acts of kindness or long-term systematic actions of intervention, "the most important thing is the offer."[7] The offer we make to others of our time and ourselves is analogous to the sacrificial offer Christ makes to each of us.

As we wrap up this brief study of personality-based evangelism styles, there is one more point to make. These styles clearly address the four geographical and cultural areas Christ commands us to reach with the gospel in Acts 1:8:

- Jerusalem, Peter at Pentecost: our town
- Judea, Andrew and Philip (with Nathanael): our county or state
- Samaria, woman at the well: state next door
- The ends of the earth, Philip (with the Ethiopian) and Paul: foreign country

Understanding this style and all the styles and using them in complement to our wiring by God makes our evangelistic efforts natural and effective. The next chapters will help you to know which styles comprise your personality.

NOTES

1. Lon Allison and Mark Anderson, *Going Public with the Gospel* (Downers Grove, IL: InterVarsity Press, 2004), 77.

2. R. Larry Moyer, *31 Days with the Master Fisherman* (Grand Rapids: Kregel Publications, 1997), 24.

3. Others have called it primarily Servant Evangelism, made famous by Pastor Steve Sjogren of the Vineyard Church in Cincinnati, Ohio. I respectfully disagree with his terminology. What he calls "Servant," I call "Service" because of the distinct nature of the actions involved.

4. Scott Wilkins, *Reach: A Team Approach to Evangelism and Assimilation* (Grand Rapids: Baker Books, 2005), 78.

5. Steve Sjogren, Dave Ping, and Doug Pollock, *Irresistible Evangelism* (Loveland, CO: Group Publishing, 2003), 92.

6. Charles L. Roesel and Donald A. Atkinson, *Meeting Needs, Sharing Christ* (Nashville: Broadman and Holman, 1995), 26.

7. Sjogren, Ping, and Pollock, 2.

CHAPTER 8

the personal assessment

This *Got Style?* Assessment was developed to help people gain insight into how they engage the world and how they can correlate that information to do evangelism in a way that complements how they have been wired by God. Our study of personalities should not be used for self-analysis only, but used to also make us more understanding of the natural inclinations and receptivity of others.

This instrument is not meant to be a personality inventory that can be relied upon to probe the inner workings of a person's mind or emotions. This inventory is not to be seen as scientifically valid.

Instructions

Record your responses to each of the thirty-six statements below on the lines before the numbers.

Answer each question according to whether or not you think the statement accurately applies to you.

Do not spend a lot of time thinking about each statement; go with your immediate reaction or gut feeling.

Use the following scale:

3 Very much like me (true 75 percent of the time)
2 Somewhat like me (true 50 percent of the time)
1 Very little like me (true 25 percent of the time)
0 Not at all like me (never true)

_____ 1. In conversations, I like to speak my mind without much small talk or beating around the bush.

_____ 2. I have a hard time getting out of bookstores or libraries without getting a bunch of books.

_____ 3. I often tell stories about my personal experiences in order to illustrate my point.

_____ 4. I am a people person who believes friendship is one of the most important things in life.

_____ 5. When I make plans to do things, I really like including or adding new people.

_____ 6. I see needs in people's lives that others often overlook.

_____ 7. I do not shy away from putting a person on the spot in a conversation when I think it is necessary.

_____ 8. I tend to analyze things and think things through.

_____ 9. I often identify with others by using phrases like "I used to think that, too" or "I have felt that way before."

_____ 10. People tell me that I make new friends easily.

_____ 11. To be honest, even if I feel I know the answers, I would rather have someone else who I think is more knowledgeable explain things to others.

_____ 12. Helping other people in tangible ways helps me feel good.

_____ 13. I believe in being completely truthful with my friends. I do not have a problem confronting my friends with the truth, even if it could hurt the relationship.

_____ 14. In conversations, I like to ask people questions about what they believe and why they believe it.

_____ 15. When I tell stories, I find people are interested in what I say and the way I say it.

_____ 16. I would rather talk to people about what is going on in their lives than discuss and discover the details of their beliefs.

_____ 17. If I knew of a good event that my friends would enjoy, I would really work hard to get them to attend it with me.

_____ 18. I prefer to express love through my actions rather than through my words.

_____ 19. I believe that real love often means telling the truth, even when it hurts.

_____ 20. I enjoy discussions and debates on difficult questions and controversial issues.

_____ 21. I intentionally share my mistakes with others when it will help them relate to the solutions I have found and hopefully avoid making the same errors.

_____ 22. I prefer getting into discussions concerning a person's life before dealing with the details of his or her beliefs.

_____ 23. I tend to go to events with other people whom I have actually invited.

_____ 24. I believe that showing people I care through my actions will make them more likely to want to listen to what I have to say.

_____ 25. A motto that would fit me is, "Make a difference or make a mess, but do something."

_____ 26. I often get frustrated with people when they use weak arguments or poor logic.

_____ 27. People seem interested in hearing stories about the things that have happened in my life.

_____ 28. I enjoy long talks as well as long walks with my friends.

_____ 29. Often when I read, hear, or see something that I really like, I immediately think of the other people I know who would enjoy it, appreciate it, or get something out of it.

_____ 30. I feel more comfortable doing something practical for someone than getting into philosophical discussions.

_____ 31. I sometimes get in trouble for the abrupt and insensitive way I interact with others.

_____ 32. I like to get at the underlying reasons for the opinions people hold and why they believe the things they do.

_____ 33. Thinking about what has happened in my life really makes me want to tell others about it.

_____ 34. People generally consider me to be a friendly, sensitive, and caring kind of person.

_____ 35. A highlight of my week would be to go somewhere special and invite someone to go along with me.

_____ 36. I'd rather work with my hands than with my head.

Transfer each statement's value to the grid provided below, totaling each column from top to bottom and then a cumulative total from left to right.

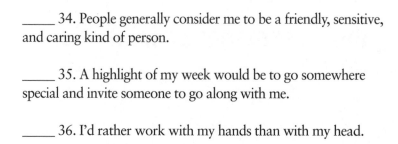

1.	2.	3.	4.	5.	6.	
7.	8.	9.	10.	11.	12.	
13.	14.	15.	16.	17.	18.	
19.	20.	21.	22.	23.	24.	
25.	26.	27.	28.	29.	30.	
31.	32.	33.	34.	35.	36.	
TOTALS ___	___	___	___	___	___	___

Table 1

Adapted from youth and adult inventories in *Becoming A Contagious Christian* (Grand Rapids: Zondervan, 1995, 2001), 15–18 (Adult) © 1995; 16–18 (Youth) © 2001.

CHAPTER 9

the assessment explanation

Simply put, Got Style?® allows the following to occur for individuals and churches:

- Relieves guilt about evangelism
- Helps people overcome feelings of inadequacy and incapacity
- Leads people from maintenance-mode to missional-mode thinking (see Postscript for Church Leaders)
- Seeks to involve the whole (local church) body in ways that complement and do not compete with the overall personality wiring of the congregation
- Allows the Holy Spirit to work in our lives in normal, natural, and nonthreatening ways

There is a three-fold key to successfully utilizing the premises of Got Style?®: education, evaluation, and explanation. Chapters 2–7 provide education about the various styles and substyles; Chapter 8 offers an assessment tool; and this chapter, Chapter 9, provides explanations for the outcomes and scores in the assessment.

Individual Scoring and Categories

Below is a sample grid. (Note: If you do the assessment with a group, you may omit the grid, in order to prevent possible tweaking by the individual group members—either consciously or subconsciously—especially if people begin to see a linear pattern to their responses.)

Name: Jane Smith, First Baptist Church, Anytown, USA

STYLE #1	STYLE #2	STYLE #3	STYLE #4	STYLE #5	STYLE #6	
1. 3	2. 1	3. 3	4. 3	5. 2	6. 2	
7. 2	8. 2	9. 1	10. 3	11. 1	12. 2	
13. 2	14. 2	15. 3	16. 2	17. 1	18. 1	
19. 2	20. 3	21. 3	22. 2	23. 1	24. 3	
25. 1	26. 2	27. 3	28. 3	29. 3	30. 1	
31. 2	32. 3	33. 2	34. 3	35. 2	36. 1	
12	**13**	**15**	**16**	**10**	**10**	**76**

Adaptation of Mark Mittelberg and Bill Hybels, *Becoming A Contagious Christian* (Grand Rapids: Zondervan, 1995), 15–18.

As noted in the directions for Chapter 8, the assessment is scored by adding the six columns vertically to obtain a total for each. These columns represent the six styles. The styles are based on personality, not spiritual giftedness. Since this adapted instrument does not contain any religious words or phrases, the responses are representative of the conscious or subconscious way a person engages the world in general. In the example, Jane Smith engages her world primarily through the means of the relational and storytelling styles and can be equipped to use these styles to share her faith in natural and effective ways.

You may also go ahead and add together the column totals in the bottom row (left to right). This will give you a cumulative score that we will discuss below under "Three Categories of Evangelism."

Styles of Strength and Styles of Leaning

The highest number that can be reached in any given column is eighteen. Any score over fifteen (83 percent of eighteen) in a column is considered a style of strength—a style that you will function in naturally and strongly. Any score within the range of eleven to fourteen (61 percent of eighteen) is a style of leaning. This means a person shows potential confidence and competence in this area if properly equipped with additional reading, classroom training, and hands-on experience. I re-assessed the scores for a person I trained recently in the Midwest, utilizing this same instrument. His outcomes went up by 50 percent because of this kind of reading, training, and experiential learning. Scores of ten or less should be disregarded for purposes of evangelism.

There is conflicting thought about where we should focus our energy in order to improve. Some believe that building on strengths will, by default, improve weak areas because they are pulled up together. Others hold that focusing on weaknesses will bring overall improvement. What matters most here is this: Evangelism is effective when you are genuine and authentic about yourself in the way God has wired you.

Three Categories of Evangelism

Evangelists

Evangelists comprise the first category of people who do evangelism. I would be the first to concede that, though evangelists tell people the Good News, they often get a bad rap. However, the assertive methods can raise a level of curiosity about Christ and the Christian faith. Being an evangelist does not mean a person has high numbers in each column; rather, he or she has the highest score (primary strength) with a seventeen or eighteen in the assertive style column, while in the other categories, he or she often has much lower numbers. Fewer people than you might think score in this way. Some authors have estimated that between 5 percent and 10 percent of Christians are evangelists in the traditional assertive style.[1] In 2001, only 6 percent of clergy felt they had the ability of an evangelist.[2] Throughout my years of work with actual outcomes from hundreds of assessments with thousands of participants (done across the country and even across cultures), I have found that the number is no higher than 3 percent, and I may be too generous with that percentage. Even in cultures that show greater dominance in this style (because of the culture's inherent ways of interaction and traditions of communication), I have not found the percentage higher than 3 percent.

One megachurch in our country, often cited as a model of an evangelizing church (heavily into the assertive methodology), claims nine thousand members. Each week, three hundred of its members are involved in planned, door-to-door outreach.[3] Since the average church in America is 120 times smaller than this megachurch, three hundred people involved in evangelism is amazing. Many congregations (and their pastors) desire to have those numbers. But do some simple math. Three hundred is only 3 percent of nine thousand. Praise the Lord for the three hundred, but what about the nearly 97 percent of the rest of them, and the rest of us? The Great Commission was never intended to be done in a way that it became The Great Omission, leaving so many out of the process and experience. The early church did not rely on trained evangelists or on trained anybody for that matter. They simply relied on people who had had a personal encounter with Christ to share their faith with those who had yet to have the same experience.

One congregation's assessment had a disproportionate number of people who scored very high in the assertive style. However, many of the church's assertive evangelistic efforts met with dismal results.

Further inquiry revealed that a former pastor, who was very high in the assertive style, had used an assertive-oriented curriculum called Evangelism Explosion (see Appendix C) to train a large percentage of the laity. While the folks understood all too well the mechanics of the methodology and could respond accordingly, they did not believe in its use and were not committed to its process. While assertive evangelism is still relevant and as effective today as in any era of the church,[4] "as a general rule, this approach should be considered an abnormal rather normal witness experience."[5]

Gift of Evangelism

The gift of evangelism comprises the second category. Doing evangelism comes quite naturally to a person who scores high across the spectrum of styles, regardless of setting or circumstances. In terms of this assessment, it means an individual has at least a fifteen in each of the six columns, indicating that the person is able to operate with confidence and competence in a variety of settings across the spectrum of evangelistic experiences. The highest score anyone can get for the entire instrument is 108 (six columns times eighteen possible points). Added from left to right, a cumulative total over ninety (eighty-third percentile or higher) gives a good indication that a person is able to operate fairly effectively in all styles. This person is able to not only communicate the gospel effectively to the unsaved in a variety of ways, but also has the ability to effectively equip the saints for the work of evangelism.

As many as 4 percent of Christians have the gift of evangelism. Perhaps. This is slightly higher than for those who are evangelists. One report says that only 1 percent of Christians who consider themselves born-again or saved believe they have the gift of evangelism.[6]

This gift is not to be confused with assertive methods such as Evangelism Explosion, through which all believers may gain some boldness or tools to evangelize. The person with the gift of evangelism looks for areas where the need for the gospel is the greatest and will personally sacrifice to meet those needs on many levels and in a variety of ways. I believe the distinction between the method and the gift is the difference between a call to evangelism and the gift of evangelism. People are effective when they operate in complement to their personality styles and not in competition with them.

Saying there is no such gift, as some do, allows people to escape responsibility. "The Bible clearly teaches there is a gift of evangelism, but that is where the clarity stops."[7] Evangelism is expected of every Christian; it is not optional. *How* we do evangelism is.

Evangelizers

Evangelists represent 3 percent of believers and rank high in the assertive style. Those with the gift of evangelism represent another 4 percent and have a high score overall. So where does that leave the overwhelming majority who do not score high in either of these first two categories? Evangelizers comprise the third and largest category. Most Christians, well over 90 percent, will have their highest scores (their primary strengths) in one or maybe two styles (analytical through incarnational). We have completed many hundreds of church assessments, representing many thousands of congregants, in English- and Spanish-language churches and inclusive of other ethnicities in the United States and Puerto Rico. These assessments show that the vast majority (one third to one half) have relational and/or incarnational styles as their primary and secondary styles. Few of us are entirely one personality style. We are mixtures, which defines our uniqueness. Three out of four people we meet will have a different personality pattern [style] than our own.[8]

Once we discover and develop our own styles, we become very effective in introducing people to Christ. Confidence comes with competence. Our particular personality isn't something to be cured or changed; rather, it is something to be celebrated.[9] We recognize God's strength is demonstrated in our personalities, not in our trying to change them.

Let me point out this important fact: Every evangelist is an evangelizer, but not every evangelizer is an evangelist. The commonly held attitude that "every Christian is an evangelist" is not true.[10] Only some of the Body of Christ are designated by God as evangelists (assertive style). However, every believer, evangelist or not, is called to be an evangelizer. Though there are only three specific scripture references to *evangelist,* there are 120 references to all members of the church sharing the gospel.[11] In other words, of these 123 verses, 2.5 percent pertain to evangelists and 98.5 percent pertain to everyone else, further supporting the distribution of personalities as I have presented.

Regardless of the given styles of strength, all methods of evangelism need to intentionally connect with others. If just saying the right thing were enough, Jesus would have showed up, taught what was needed, and moved on. But Jesus stayed around for a while and was moved with compassion by the needs he encountered. He made a difference. He was a life-changer. Conversely, if living a good life were a sufficient witness, Jesus would have just shown up and would have done good for everyone. That should have accomplished the goal, because no one could live better than Christ. But Jesus didn't; he spent a lot of time teaching the multitudes and individuals. To be an evangelistic follower of Jesus is to both *say* and *do.*

Group Scoring and Congregational "Personality"

If the assessment is to be an accurate reflection of the congregation, it must be taken by as many of the active adult church members as possible, or at least by a very good cross-section of the congregation (30 percent of average Sunday morning attendance). Then the church might set a goal of testing three-fourths of the active adult resident membership within a three-year period. Follow up with a reminder to members who have not yet taken the inventory. For new believers, participation in the process becomes a standard practice in all new member classes.

To use the assessment information corporately, take each assessment grid, as in the example below, and determine the participant's primary style (highest score) as well as his or her secondary style (second-highest score) of strength.

Name: Jane Smith (Sample), First Baptist Church, Anytown, USA

STYLE #1	STYLE #2	STYLE #3	STYLE #4	STYLE #5	STYLE #6	
1. 3	2. 1	3. 3	4. 3	5. 2	6. 2	
7. 2	8. 2	9. 1	10. 3	11. 1	12. 2	
13. 2	14. 2	15. 3	16. 2	17. 1	18. 1	
19. 2	20. 3	21. 3	22. 2	23. 1	24. 3	
25. 1	26. 2	27. 3	28. 3	29. 3	30. 1	
31. 2	32. 3	33. 2	34. 3	35. 2	36. 1	
12	**13**	**⑮**	**⑯**	**10**	**10**	**76**

↑ Secondary Style   ↑ Primary Style

You can glean each person's scores from their individual grid, or you can move all the participants' column totals to a sheet. (See sample on next page.) Get a visual compilation of scores by highlighting primary and secondary scores before you move forward.

	Name	Assertive	Analytical	Storytelling	Relational	Invitational	Incarnational	Total	Designation
1	Kim	13	12	14	(15)	10	(15)	79	Evangelizer
2	Charmagne	14	(16)	14	14	10	(17)	85	Evangelizer
3	Jonathan	12	(14)	10	13	9	(15)	73	Evangelizer
4	Carver	5	11	12	(17)	8	(15)	68	Evangelizer
5	Sally	7	8	7	(14)	9	(17)	62	Evangelizer
6	David	5	(12)	10	(13)	12	11	63	Evangelizer
7	Phillip	(14)	5	(14)	13	10	(14)	70	Evangelizer
8	Ben	15	15	(17)	18	(17)	16	98	Gift of Evangelism
9	Susan #1	14	14	12	16	(17)	(17)	90	Evangelizer
10	Marge	9	14	13	(16)	(16)	(14)	82	Evangelizer
11	Isabelle	8	(17)	15	16	15	(18)	89	Evangelizer
12	James	(17)	12	12	14	13	(16)	84	Evangelist
13	Susan #2	8	11	11	(13)	(13)	(16)	72	Evangelizer
14	Olive	13	14	(15)	13	11	(16)	82	Evangelizer
15	Jane	12	13	(15)	(16)	10	10	76	Evangelizer

To have an accurate picture of the congregation, be sure to plot each participant in more than one style, if possible. If the primary score occurs in more than one style, plot just the primary scores, numerous as they may be. If there is only one highest number, plot the secondary style also.

Next move the name of each person from his or her grid to what I call the Plot Chart, as shown below. Be sure to put the person's name and his or her value in each style. (See chart on next page.)

How to Approach Got Style?® Training

At this point, a decision has to be made about the next step in the overall Got Style?® strategy. You can decide to do training in each of the six styles OR you can do a "styles reduction." This decision is based on how many people need training and how many people can do the training. Not all churches have time and treasure enough to provide training for everyone in every style. This is the reality in smaller churches. In addition, the point person is often the pastor. If the pastor does not have the gift of evangelism—i.e., high scores across all styles—he or she will need to spend a lot of time and energy reading and retaining information to disseminate to others. Also, the congregation will have to set aside a lot of time to make itself available for the training. Each curriculum spans four weeks and can average $75 per kit or $450 to cover all six styles. Some curriculums require more time; some cost more money. Most churches just don't have that kind of time and money. It is an issue of stewardship of resources—evangelism that never happens is poor stewardship.

So to get the biggest bang for the time and effort spent, getting the most people in the fewest styles (styles reduction) may be the best way to go. The reduction would work as follows in the sample below. Use checks or slash marks to indicate that people can be plotted in other styles. There is no right or wrong way to do this

BEFORE STYLES REDUCTION

	Incarnational	Invitational	Relational	Storytelling	Analytical	Assertive
1	Kim (15)	David (12)	Kim (15)	Phillip (14)	Charmagne (16)	Phillip (14)
2	Charmagne (17)	Ben (17)	Carver (17)	Ben (17)	Jonathan (15)	James (17)
3	Jonathan (15)	Susan #1 (17)	Sally (14)	Olive (15)	David (12)	
4	Carver (15)	Marge (16)	David (13)	Jane (15)	Isabelle (17)	
5	Sally (17)	Susan #2 (13)	Ben (18)			
6	Phillip (14)		Marge (16)			
7	Susan #1 (17)		Susan #2 (13)			
8	Isabelle (18)		Jane (16)			
9	James (16)					
10	Susan #2 (16)					
11	Olive (16)					

AFTER STYLES REDUCTION

	Assertive	Analytical	Storytelling	Relational	Invitational	Incarnational	
1	~~Phillip (14)~~	~~Charmagne (16)~~	~~Phillip (14)~~	*Kim (15)*	~~David (12)~~	Kim (15)	1
2	~~James (17)~~	~~Jonathan (14)~~	~~Ben (17)~~	*Carver (17)*	~~Ben (17)~~	Charmagne (17)	2
3		~~David (12)~~	~~Olive (15)~~	*Sally (14)*	~~Susan #1 (17)~~	Jonathan (15)	3
4		~~Isabelle (17)~~	~~Jane (15)~~	David (13)	~~Marge (16)~~	Carver (15)	4
5				Ben (18)	~~Susan #2 (13)~~	Sally (17)	5
6				Marge (16)		Phillip (14)	6
7				*Susan #2 (13)*		Susan #1 (17)	7
8				Jane (16)		Isabelle (18)	8
9						James (16)*	9
10						Susan #2 (16)	10
11						Olive (16)	11

reduction, but it does make sense to work with the styles with the fewest number of people, noting if participants are found in other styles with equal or higher scores. Below, italicized names indicate people who appear in more than one column and are doubly covered with dominant styles. (See p. 129.)

From the Plot Chart (See p. 128.), representative of a Sunday School class in any given church, we gain the following information:

- Eleven of the fifteen participants plot under Incarnational (73 percent).
- Eight of the fifteen participants plot under Relational (53 percent).
- Fifteen of the fifteen participants plot under *either* Incarnational and Relational (100 percent).
- Four of the fifteen participants plot under *both* Incarnational *and* relational (26 percent) with their primary and secondary styles.
- One participant plots as an evangelist. Individual mentoring is the best method to equip this person for evangelism. Note that this individual does also plot under Incarnational with just a point difference from his score under Incarnational, which is considered statistically insignificant.

We have been able to reduce all participants for inclusion into two styles, incarnational and relational. These would be considered the group's Primary Collective Style and the Secondary Collective Style, respectively. Everyone who is plotted in either of these two styles is working within his or her Primary Individual Style, which as you will remember indicates his or her highest score. Of the sampling, ten participants are working in within a style of strength (a score of fifteen or higher), and three are working within a style of leaning (a score of eleven to fifteen), with each of the three scores in the upper end of the specified range.

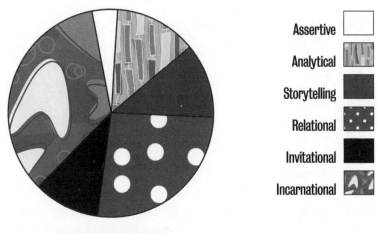

Assertive
Analytical
Storytelling
Relational
Invitational
Incarnational

BEFORE STYLES REDUCTION

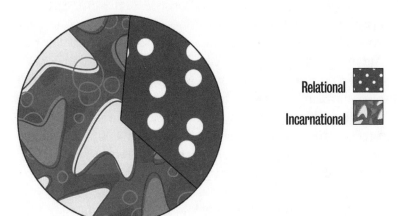

Relational
Incarnational

AFTER STYLES REDUCTION

So, instead of the pastor or core lay leader having to assimilate and then disseminate six different curriculums, she only needs to learn two and ends up with 100 percent coverage of the sampling, if everyone participates.

I would be the first to confess that not all styles-reduction plot charts will turn out this neatly. But of the many hundreds I have done, most do. Sometimes, especially in larger samplings, people appear all over the place with all kinds of scores. If the church is large, training can be provided across the entire spectrum of styles, because there are sufficient trainers and trainees for each style to make the effort worthwhile. In these congregations, reduction is not imperative or even helpful. I worked with a large African American congregation outside of Philadelphia that conducted three hours of simultaneous training in each of the six styles on a certain Saturday. All six sessions were held in the morning and repeated in the afternoon, allowing participants to go to sessions focused on their primary and secondary styles or to select specific sessions if they had equal values in more than one style. Also, individuals could decide to go to sessions that focused on their assessed weaknesses, hoping that by equipping those areas, scores would improve. Another possibility is that several churches can join together, sharing responsibilities and resources as well as bolstering the number of participants. I coordinated this kind of effort with a dozen churches in Montana. They came together from around the state to a central location on a Saturday and provided simultaneous training. Included were classroom instruction, hands-on experience, and a time of debriefing and celebration afterwards.

Team Formation within Congregations

Let me again say that all the styles are valid forms of evangelism, just distinct and different from one another. However, it is my conviction that true missional evangelism involves a team concept and component. A team approach increases the odds of effective evangelism by helping believers match their evangelistic style to the nature of the person they are seeking to influence.[12] Instead of just a few people giving spiritual birth, the whole Body of Christ gets to be involved. Evangelists are meant to work with the church, not as a substitute for it. Since holistic evangelism involves both words and works, there needs to be a balance of people with varying primary styles working together to share Christ with others. Christians working together for one common goal is a strong witness in itself.[13] Working together not only keeps the givers of the gospel balanced in the way they present Christ, it always makes what is done for the receivers more personal. The wider the variety of styles, the wider the reach we have for Christ.[14]

Neither society nor the church could operate without a multiplicity of personalities. Because believers and receivers have different styles and send and receive differently, style-based evangelism has both a giver and receiver sensitivity. We need to be bilingual in regard to the styles. We need to speak out of our own innate style and speak intentionally to the personality styles of others. Styles in people are not isolated and often overlap; this, in fact, provides a complementary synergy. Indeed, God designed each of us to be most effective with certain people, mostly those who are wired as we are, with a composition of personalities that complement our own. "Though all aspects of God listed in the Bible are accurate, from our own particular personalities, we identify with certain parts more than others do."[15] Obviously, it is true that our personalities affect how we interact with one another.

As individuals have styles that complement one another, looking at complementary styles is needed for evangelistic teamwork. As Christians work with each other and ensure the styles are adequately represented, this group becomes the natural support system for lifelong discipleship, starting at conversion. The team experience allows one style to call upon another style to speak into a person's experience in a style-specific and style-strong way. "A cause for a weakened evangelistic enterprise is the imbalance between the verbalization [words] and the incarnation [works] of the gospel."[16] When the team concept is employed, it is harder for people to point out one

Christian's fault, since their encounters with Christianity become a group experience. Of course, it takes time to build quality teams. But remember that while Jesus had three years to lay out his plan to save the world, the first thing he did was build a team.

Actual outreach comes naturally as people discover their styles and then are put together either with like-minded congregants (homogenous team) or mixed styles (eclectic team) and are allowed to dream up what they will do. In fact, the dream often determines the formation of the team. The leadership provides style-specific training for the group that is experientially based. People are allowed to create their own outreach, either as a small group or for the whole of the church. Since participants are empowered to birth their own outreach, no buy-in is required. Obviously this approach depends upon the size of the church and the size of the group within a larger church who are committed to participating. "The New Testament pattern is a blend of proclamation and the practical meeting of needs."[17] Therefore, the best strategy for balance is to create an eclectic team composed of the various styles. This way we build on one another's strengths and compensate for one another's weaknesses.

Resources

I have written this book in small part to fill what I perceive to be a gap that exists between the book *Becoming a Contagious Christian* by Bill Hybels and Mark Mittleberg (theory) and its sequel, *Building a Contagious Church* by Mark Mittleberg (practice), the definitive resources on outreach ideas actually being used in churches across the country and across the spectrum of styles. Part of filling the gap is providing an annotated recommended resource for each of the styles and substyles (Appendix B).

NOTES

1. From his empirical evidence in 1979, Peter Wagner believed about 10 percent of the Body of Christ has this assertive evangelistic bent. In the 1990s Christian

Schwarz affirmed this statistic in his book, *Natural Church Development* (Carol Stream, IL: ChurchSmart Resources, 1996). Though without empirical data to prove the finding, Bruce Roberts Dreisbach reaffirmed it in his book, *The Jesus Plan* (Colorado Springs: WaterBrook Press, 2002). In *Lifestyle Evangelism*, Joe Aldrich doubts that 10 percent will ever be effective in this type of evangelism (Portland, OR: Multnomah Press, 2006), and Lon Allison noted the percentage to be as low as 5 percent in the book he coauthored with Mark Anderson, *Going Public with the Gospel* (Downers Grove, IL: InterVarsity Press, 2004).

2. George Barna, *The Habits of Highly Effective Churches* (Ventura, CA: Regal/Gospel Light Publications, 1998), 32.

3. Aldrich, 211.

4. Allison and Anderson, 49.

5. Aldrich, 76.

6. Gary D. Foster, compiler and editor, "News and Trends," *Evangelism Connection,* March 2009, http://web.memberclicks.com/mc/getLink.do?id=743241041136962413811BD1P&linkId=4647 (accessed March 19, 2009).

7. G. Michael Cocoris, *Evangelism: A Biblical Approach* (Kearney, NE: Moody Publishing, 1984), 95.

8. Jard DeVille, *The Psychology of Witnessing* (Waco, TX: Word Books, 1980), 56.

9. Mike Bechtle, *Evangelism for the Rest of Us* (Grand Rapids: Baker Books, 2006), 29.

10. Schwarz, 34.

11. Win Arn and Charles Arn, *The Master's Plan for Making Disciples,* (Grand Rapids: Baker Books, 1998), 27-28.

12. Barna, 117.

13. Helen Boursier, *Tell It with Style* (Downers Grove, IL: InterVarsity Press, 1995), 163.

14. Boursier, 117.

15. Marita Littauer, *Your Spiritual Personality* (San Francisco: Jossey-Bass, 2004), 40.

16. Tom Clegg and Warren Bird, *Lost in America* (Loveland, CO: Group Publishing, 2001), 73.

17. Aldrich, 127.

postscript for church leaders
the maintenance mindset vs.
the missional mindset

If you have just finished reading this book for the first time and are tempted now to leap into an assessment and training with your congregation as soon as possible, then please STOP! You need to back up and build a foundation for this work. Any congregation embarking on evangelism needs to deal first with its own spiritual health. The evidence of spiritual health in a congregation is the birthing of spiritually healthy individuals and also other spiritually healthy congregations. Spiritual health here is equal to a missional mindset. Individuals and churches doing evangelism to save others, viewing it as a step in growing mature followers of Christ are *missional*. Individuals and churches doing evangelism to save themselves and as a means to perpetuate an institution have a *maintenance* mindset. So the question that must be asked is this: Do you have a missional or a maintenance mindset?

There is much discussion today about the missional church. This dialogue must be rooted in the Word of God and demonstrated in the life of Christ, the greatest of all missional examples. To contrast the mindsets of missional and maintenance churches, we will look at what I consider to be the most familiar of all Jesus' miracles, the Feeding of the Five Thousand-Plus. This is the only miracle besides Christ's own resurrection that is repeated in each of the four Gospels. Melding these four accounts together with their different perspectives gives us the most complete picture of what happened that particular day on the Sea of Galilee. What follows is my own compilation of this miracle, as translated in the New International Version of the Holy Bible. This will serve as the biblical basis for our discussion about the missional mindset and church. As my publisher Laura Alden says, may you find something new in the familiar and something familiar in the new.

Feeding of the Five Thousand-plus

Jesus crossed to the far shore of the Sea of Galilee. A great crowd of	John 6:1
people followed him because they saw the miraculous signs he had	John 6:2
performed on the sick. He welcomed them and spoke to them about	Luke 9:11
the Kingdom of God. Having compassion upon them, he healed	Mark 6:34
those among them who needed healing.	Luke 9:11

Late in the afternoon, the disciples came to him and said, "This is a	Luke 9:12
remote place here, and it's already getting very late. Send the crowds	Matthew 14:15
away so they can go to the villages and buy themselves more food to	Mark 6:36
eat and find lodging." When Jesus looked up and saw a great crowd	John 6:5a
coming toward him, he responded, "They do not need to go away.	John 6b
You give them something to eat." He then said to Philip, "Where	Mark 6:36
shall we buy bread for these people to eat?" He asked this only to test	John 6:5
him, for he already had in mind what he was going to do. Philip an-	John 6:6
swered him, "Eight months' of a man's wages would not buy enough	John 6:7
bread for each one to have a bite! Are we to go and spend that much	Mark 6:37a
on bread and give it to them to eat.	Mark 6:37b

"How many loaves do you have?" Jesus asked. "Go and see."	Mark 6:38a
When they found out, another of his disciples, Andrew, Simon	Mark 6:38b
Peter's brother, spoke up, "Here is a boy with just five small barley	John 6:9a
loaves and two small fish, but how far will they go among so	John 6:9b
many?" "Bring them here to me," Jesus said.	Matthew 14:18

Jesus directed the disciples to have all the people sit down in	Mark 6:39
groups on the expanses of green grass in that place. Five thou-	John 6:10
sand men besides the women and children sat down in groups of	Matthew 14:21
hundreds and fifties.	Mark 6:40

Jesus then took the loaves and two fish, and looking up to heaven,	Mark 6:41
gave thanks and broke the loaves. Then he gave them to the disci-	Luke 9:16
ples and the disciples gave them to those who were seated as much	Matthew 14:19
as they wanted. He did the same with the fish.	John 6:11

When they had all had enough to eat, he said to his disciples,	John 6:12
"Gather the pieces that are left over. Let nothing be wasted." So they	John 6:13
gathered them and filled twelve baskets with the pieces of the five	Matthew 14:20
barley loaves left and fish over by those who had eaten.	Mark 6:43

(Mark 6:34-44, Matthew 14:15-21, Luke 9:11-14, John 6:1-13)

I modify the traditional title of the text, calling it "The Feeding of the Five Thousand-*Plus*" because the passage clearly states that there were five thousand men, not counting the women and children. If just half of these men had brought their wives along for the day, there were seven thousand five hundred people. If those couples had just one kid in tow, the crowd swelled to at least ten thousand. A number of Bible scholars place the crowd that afternoon somewhere between fifteen and twenty thousand people. As such, this was the largest miracle recorded that Jesus performed, impacting the most number of people in one place at one time. Present that day were young and old, singles and married folks, men and women, boys and girls, mostly Jews, and probably even some Gentiles. The crowd was a microcosm of humanity. Yet at that moment, few if any in the crowd knew they would be direct recipients of the miracle-working power of Jesus to provide for basic needs.

One fact of life is that day-to-day things—eating, drinking, and such—consume our time, energy, and resources. Evangelism is done even as other things vie for our time and attention. Jesus experienced the same tension. Feeding of the five thousand-plus was not the only thing that happened that day in Jesus' or the disciples' lives. Earlier, Jesus had sent his disciples out to minister in pairs. They had come back both exhilarated and exhausted. In addition, Jesus had heard that his relative, friend, and colleague—John—had been put to an unjustifiable and tragic death. Now Jesus also had learned that the same guy who had put John to death would like to "have a meeting" with Jesus, probably with similar and suspect motives. Overshadowing all of that, the Jewish Passover feast was near with its special preparations. If Jesus had waited for the perfect, uninterrupted time, free of distractions and other responsibilities, this miracle never would have occurred.

Jesus' response to life's turmoil was to tell his disciples, "We just need some time away." He led them to the far side of the Sea of Galilee. However, the crowds, who could see from one side to the other, followed the shoreline and met him as he disembarked. Life for Jesus, as for us, did not happen as planned. In spite of this interruption to the planned getaway, Jesus' immediate reaction to the crowd was compassion. The text states Jesus sat down and taught them. Sitting down indicated his intention to spend quality and quantitative time with them. So if we are looking for the right moment when things calm down in order to address maintenance and missional issues and to attend to evangelism, that day will never come. A missional mindset is motivated by compassion for others. A maintenance mindset is moved by concern for oneself.

The initial miracle is that Jesus could get them all to sit down, to be quiet, and to listen—for *hours*. Even though Jesus taught for the better part of a day, nothing of what he said has been recorded in any of the four accounts. Not one word. That is intriguing in light of the fact that in a similar setting, maybe in the same geographic spot on an earlier occasion, Jesus' every word was written down in Matthew 5–7, traditionally referred to as the Sermon on the Mount. It seems possible Jesus' words were not recorded here because the disciples were not listening. Perhaps, as one of my colleagues said, the reason Jesus' teaching was omitted was because people tend to always remember what you do, though they may not remember what you say.

So if the apostles were not listening to Jesus, what were they doing? It seems they had a quasi-committee meeting and, after reaching their decision, shared their collective wisdom with him. "We have decided *you* should send the crowd away." Here is a first key distinction between the missional and the maintenance mindset: The first looks to thrive while the second is happy to survive. In the life of the church, we see a missional mindset at work in teams to make disciples as they operate in complement to their personalities. Missional churches attempt to embrace situations and see their potential, while acknowledging the difficulty they represent. Personal involvement is high.

By contrast, the maintenance mindset it focused on forming committees that make decisions, not disciples. Serving on boards or committees becomes the ministry, not merely the means to get ministry done well. Committees and boards use words like *we* and *us* to represent a larger or stronger constituency than themselves—one that usually does not exist. Maintenance churches attempt to distance themselves from potential problems. Why? They are in meetings and have no time. They believe that if they distance themselves far enough away from the reality of the problems of people's lives, those problems might just go away. That is exactly what the disciples asked for. They asked Jesus to send the crowd—i.e., the problem—far, far away. Personal involvement is low.

Please note that the result of the disciples' committee meeting was to tell Jesus what to do. The disciples had a right theology because they believed Jesus had the miraculous power to control and command a crowd that numbered into the thousands, because he had already proven he could. They did not, however, believe Jesus could do anything for them like miraculously feeding them. Fend them off, yes. Feed them, no. The possibility never entered their thinking. Another distinction between missional and maintenance mindsets is that a maintenance mindset tells the Lord what to do; a missional mindset does what the Lord says. Right theology or orthodoxy does not necessarily mean right practice or outcomes. In the words of emergent church leader Brian McLaren, "orthodoxy does not equate with orthopraxy."[1] Jesus said it first when he warned his followers about the Pharisees: "listen to what they say [theology], but do not follow their example [practice]" (Matthew 23:3).

Back to the hungry crowd. The passage records that Jesus already had in mind what he was going to do. So when the disciples attempted to force their agenda on Jesus by saying, "You send them away," Jesus said, "No. That's not how it's going to happen." I can hear the discussion in my mind. The disciples pressed Jesus: "But we discussed it over and over—over there!" Jesus said, "That's the problem. You were over there, and I was over here. If I'm not in it, then it's not mine, and I'm not claiming it. I will not accept responsibility nor will I give approval." Jesus continued, "I never told you to do that. You should have been here with me, hearing the word of God about the kingdom of God instead of trying to establish and maintain your own idea of the kingdom, or your kingdom. You would do better identifying with the present reality instead of trying to create a separate and different one." Jesus added, "I have a better idea. No matter how many votes you got in your committee, I am a majority of one. I've decided *you* are to feed them."

Jesus expected they would depend on him for the outcome. The disciples suffered from a maintenance mindset here because they thought *they* had to create something that met with Jesus' approval. Just the thought of such responsibility incapacitated them, as it would any of us. But the missional mindset realizes God already and always has a plan. It is simply our responsibility to discern, discover, and then do it. In a missional church, everyone is or can be involved because they view themselves as doing God's work in partnership with God, not just working for God. The missional mindset believes everyone has something to offer because God has given everyone something to share. It is emancipating to live in this truth and reality.

The disciples responded to Jesus' instructions with excuses. The first but not last excuse was, "We don't have enough money. If we had more, it would solve all our problems!" The second was, "We're in a bad location. We are out here in the middle of nowhere. One time this was a real thriving area, Lord, but not now. We just don't have it going for us here; send the people into the towns and villages and let them find something there, because we don't have it to give." Their third excuse was, "It's too late. We did great things once, but that was then and this is now. Now we are just kind of passing time, but we are not passing out food. What we have, we need, and it is never enough." Simply put, they told the Lord, "This is not a good time." They found time for excuses but not for dealing with the problem. No matter what you do (or do not do), you expend energy. Deciding whether your time will be spent productively or in vain is the real decision.

Over and over again, we see the disciples of Jesus—not the crowd and not their need—being the hindrance. Those closest to Christ caused the difficulty in working out the problem and unfolding the miracle. But here we find that God makes things happen. God does not wait for things to occur. Maintenance-minded believers are always tense, always anxious, because they never know what's going to happen or how they will have to respond. They avoid engagement, doing just enough to get by. Missional-minded disciples are proactive, looking for things to do. Even though they are already doing some things, they are willing to do more, believing that since God's in it, God's sufficiency will be more than their lack of supply.

So Jesus made things happen by sending the Twelve into the crowd. The disciples needed to identify with the people (as in the relational style) and with their need (as in the incarnational style). That day, some people had wandered for days, thinking they had finally found the answer, only to find more problems. Some of us who are believers have been with other believers in our "holy huddles" for so long that we have forgotten what it is like to be lost and spiritually hungry. We have forgotten what it is like to be in that crowd. We have just forgotten. Jesus says, "The only way you will appreciate their pain, identify with their lostness and lack, and find motivation to do something is to get out among them." Maintenance believers and churches want to be attractive, getting people to come to them. Missional disciples are attracted to where the people are.

The passage says the disciples simply go, not willingly and definitely not submissively, but they go. They probably did not think it was a great way to spend the day. That, additionally, is worth noting. You do not have to want to or wait to have a really good attitude to do what God asks of you. With God, it is not so much about our attitude as it is about our availability and obedience in doing what God asks, even when we do not understand all the dynamics and particulars.

After going out among the crowd, the disciples returned with a report: "We've got *only* five loaves and two fish." Though there was little food, Scripture says there was plenty of grass in that place. If God could provide ample space for them to sit, God could provide ample food for them to eat. Every excuse the disciples made, Jesus counteracted.

So the first big problem was addressed when Jesus told the disciples, "Make the people sit down" in groups of hundreds and fifties. Jesus continued to engage the disciples in working out the miracle, not allowing them to sit on the sidelines as observers, letting Jesus do it right the first time all by himself. Jesus wanted and encouraged the disciples' involvement, even with their faults and shortcomings. While a maintenance mindset is immobilized by the size and scope of what one is called to do, a missional mindset breaks the problem down to manageable parts. Missional disciples do not try to do everything all at once because they know they cannot be everything to everyone all the time. Jesus accepts and understands our limitations. He only expects us to work with what we have and with the next person who comes our way.

Then Jesus did something that the disciples never did in this entire portion of scripture: Jesus prayed. He may have actually prayed the traditional Jewish blessing: "Blessed are you, Lord God of the universe, creator of heaven and earth, who brings forth bread from the earth." We don't know for sure what Christ said, but we know to whom he said it. He spoke to God. Here again is another distinction of missional disciples: They pray with intensity and a sense of God's presence. (A maintenance believer is more likely to pray token, thirty-second "bless me" prayers.)

Jesus then did something I will never understand. He gave the food back to the very disciples who had just tried to pawn the problem off on him! If I had been Jesus, I would have operated out of that old adage, "If you want something done right, do it yourself." I would have looked those disciples in the eyes and have said, "You have been more hindrance than help; just sit down and watch me do it." But as you know, that is not how it happened. Even when they continued to distance themselves from the crowd and the Christ, Jesus once more commissioned the Twelve to go into the crowd. The first time they went with empty hands; the second time they went with what seemed empty hands. Each disciple carried a two-gallon-sized basket with their portion of the five loaves and two fish. The loaves were about the size of a silver dollar pancake, and the fish were probably the size of a bluegill— able to fit easily in an average adult's hand. The disciples had *thousands* of stomachs to fill. No way could they have moved forward if they had not depended on the Lord, even if that dependence was half-hearted. A maintenance mindset tries to do things without

God. A missional mindset realizes it is all about dependence. God will never take us to a place of self-sufficiency. Jesus kept calling them (as he does us) to involvement, from maintenance to missional living.

Notice Jesus was the one who sat on the sideline. He did not personally feed anybody that afternoon. The disciples took the food to the crowd as Jesus had instructed and became his hands and feet (as in the incarnational style). Maintenance believers hold and hoard, thinking what they have is all they are going to get. They are probably right. There is no reason for them to get more, because they do not do what is right with what they already have been given. Missional disciples release and receive because they acknowledge that everything is the Lord's. Theirs is not a theology of give to get, but a belief of get to give. Maintenance believers do not get what missional disciples fully embrace: God's name is on the line, and God will see it through. It is not about us. It is about the crowd out there who forms the community we are called to reach. Wherever you have a chance to encounter people by divine providence—that is your community.

The crowd did not respond antagonistically to what God offered them. They literally ate it up. Our unwillingness to reach out has much less to do with how the non-Christian will respond and much more to do with our assumptions about their reactions. *We have believed our own lies.* We have told ourselves that they do not want us to interact with them, when it is probably more honest to say *we* do not want to interact with them. Maintenance believers set up a fortress, surrounding themselves with ways to keep people out. They do not want to change and do everything they can to prevent it. Missional disciples see themselves as a force for good, moving out for God. They constantly change methods in order to remain relevant and contextual, for the sake of others.

What do we make of the twelve baskets of leftovers? It was more than the disciples could have eaten themselves. So they had food for the moment and fragments for others in the future. Missional disciples see potential—with God everything happens to serve both a present and future purpose. Every person who comes to faith in Christ represents the potential of someone else also coming. Maintenance believers live primarily in the past and in fear of the future.

I want to conclude this book about evangelism by demonstrating how this passage clearly presents the elements of the gospel message, an adaptation of Ken Hemphill and Frank Harber's *Got Life?*®[2] First, we see the *love of God* expressed through the compassion of Christ. Scripture tells us eight times that Jesus was moved with compassion. He saw the crowd and was concerned about their entire well-being, physically and spiritually. Jesus could not leave them how he found them and had to do something to address their need. Since love is woven into his spiritual DNA, his response is not out of obligation nor guilt, but out of love. He knew his solution to their pressing problem was temporary, because they would need to eat again the next day. But that day he was responsible for their lives, and so he did what needed to be done.

Second, we discover the crowds' *isolation and inadequacy*. They were in a deserted place, unable to find enough food to eat. Even with their intentional efforts, what they came up with was insufficient. Third, the passage tells us the disciples surrendered their wills, were obedient to Christ's command, and turned over themselves (repentance) and what they discovered (forgiveness) to Jesus. They trusted him even if they did not understand how it was all going to work out. Jesus turned around and empowered them to do *by faith* what they otherwise could not be or do without him. Finally, the passage teaches that God provides for both the here and now as well as for the hereafter. The people had food in abundance—there was food all over the ground! There was so much that the folks did not need to be very careful about how much they grabbed to eat or how they ate it. The twelve baskets of leftovers

Missional vs. Maintenance Mindset

MISSIONAL MINDSET	MAINTENANCE MINDSET
■ Totally Thriving	■ Barely Surviving
■ Vision Casters	■ Vision Killers
■ Looks Forward	■ Looks Back
■ Engages Itself with the Culture	■ Distances itself from the culture
■ Wants to serve—"We do this for others."—Service	■ Wants to be served—"You do this for us"—Serve Us
■ Outward Looking	■ Inward Looking
■ Participant	■ Observer
■ Has Teams	■ Has committees
■ Discerns and Discovers	■ Discusses and Debates
■ Talks to the Lord	■ Talks to each other
■ Listens to the Lord	■ Listens to each other
■ Proactive	■ Reactive
■ Views meetings as a means to ministry, to meeting others' needs	■ Views meetings as ministry, an end to meeting their own needs
■ Believes God already knows what to do, they just have to ask	■ Trying to figure out what to do for God through programs
■ "They, Theirs, and There"	■ "Us, Ours, and Here"
■ Strives to Become Diverse	■ Strives to remain Homogeneous
■ Prophetic	■ Pathetic
■ The Lord tells them what to do	■ They tell the Lord what to do
■ Orthopraxy, "We're righteous."	■ Orthodoxy, "We're right"
■ High engagement	■ Low involvement
■ Makes disciples:	■ Makes excuses:
• financial: "God needs nothing to do something."	• financial: "not enough money"
• geographic: "The Lord is in our midst, so we'll be just fine."	• geographic: "bad location"
• chronological: "Today God can do a new thing."	• chronological: "too late, our day is past"
■ Remembers what it means to be lost and hurting	■ Forgotten what it means to be lost and hurting
■ Focuses on what they do have (half-full), and it is enough	■ Focuses on what they don't have (half-empty), and it is not enough
■ Realizes they only have to do what God enables them to do	■ Thinks they have to be everything to everybody
■ Breaks a problem down to manageable parts	■ Overwhelmed by the big picture and problem

MISSIONAL MINDSET continued
- Sees problems as opportunities for their faith
- Relies on the Lord, "God can do this."
- Releases, "How much can we give?" (It's all God's.)
- Force mentality: Change Agent
- Loves and serves others
- Simply put: a help to the gospel

MAINTENANCE MINDSET continued
- Sees problems as obstacles to their faith
- Relies on themselves, "We have to do this."
- Hoard, "How much can we keep?" (It's all ours.)
- Fortress mentality: status quo
- Loves and Serves Themselves
- Simply put: a hindrance to the gospel

*"Can do all things through
Christ who makes it happen"*
(Philippians 4:13)

*"Having a form of godliness,
but denying its power"*
(2 Timothy 3:5)

indicate God clearly provided *extraordinary* (here-and-now) and *eternal* (hereafter) provisions. The people did not have to understand all the dynamics to be recipients of God's grace. They just had to be willing to receive it.

This whole thing is about the prefix *co,* which means partnership—*co*mmission, *co*mmandment, *co*mmunity, *co*mpassion—disciples working together to do something for and with God that they could never do without God. We must believe God wants to do great things, and that he wants to do them *through us.* Let's get busy doing God's work, anticipating a world changed for God, one spiritual mouth at a time!

Above is a side-by-side comparison of missional and the maintenance mindset characteristics.

NOTES

1. Brian McLaren, *A Generous Orthodoxy* (Grand Rapids: Zondervan Youth Specialties, 2004), 30-31.

2. Ken Hemphill and Frank Harber, *Got Life?* (Keller, TX: HeartSpring Media, 2000). www.gotlife.org.

the details of the process

As I noted in the Preface for Leaders, personality-based evangelism styles are not stand-alone techniques, as important as they are. They are a part of a larger process in which congregations need to be involved if they are going to align or realign themselves with God's mission in the world. While people can find new joy and freedom in sharing Christ with others through discovering their styles, a more significant impact is possible when congregations in whole or in part discover and employ their styles together. In the Preface, I outlined the steps of this overall process for a congregation. Here is a brief explanation of what is involved in these steps.

Step 1: Prayer

Done by leadership (pastors and key lay leaders) who spend significant amounts of time together in prayer, seeking the Lord for discernment about what their congregation should be doing specifically to reach out to others in their local area. Although prayer should undergird the life of a congregation at all levels, this prayer continually seeks the Lord's will until it is discerned. If done with intentionality, this step can and usually does last months. In addition, some type of church health assessment should be included to discover the strengths and weaknesses of the church, so that the leadership knows where to focus time, energy, and resources to lead the congregation forward and to prepare for the evangelism that will grow out of the church's renewed vitality. Programs such as

Becoming a Healthy Church, Natural Church Development, or *Ten Strengths of US Congregations* are useful tools (see Appendix B). Often midlevel judicatories (regions, conferences, presbyteries) have resources and staff to aid a congregation in this work.

Step 2: Vision Casting

No church can do everything. It is crucial, then, that the pastors and core lay leaders convey clearly and repeatedly to the congregation God's vision for that congregation. Here, vision means the discerned and discovered-from-God purpose of a particular local church and the special kingdom-contribution work it is meant to do in its local, specific community. They intentionally spread this vision through whatever means of communication is available: the pulpit, discipleship training, newsletters, bulletins, and websites. It is also necessary that budgets and activities reflect this God-given focus; those things that do not fall in line with the focus need to be set aside or removed.

Step 3: Prayer and Hospitality Training

Although not everyone will actively participate in the actual and eventual outreach, everyone needs to be aware that the church is becoming intentional in reaching out. Thus, the church folks need to be ready to welcome and receive the new folks who will come. "The Lord added to their numbers daily" (Acts 2:41). A crucial part of this training is best done from the pulpit through a series of Sunday morning messages on Christian hospitality. Congregations often see themselves as friendly; this training seeks to move them from being friendly to offering friendship. Included are intentional, and dare I say, lengthy times of prayer throughout the church during the week. Since most churches have their highest attendance on Sunday morning, it is best to use this time to full opportunity. Prayer in this step should focus on each believer praying for a cluster of non-Christians by name over weeks and months. At the end of the specified period, there will be a change, but not always as we might anticipate. It seems as much has happened in the lives of the ones who pray as has happened in the lives of those who are prayed for, if not more. The goal of this step it to change the overall culture and outlook of the congregation from self-reflective to self-giving.

Step 4: Personality Styles Assessment

Simply put, this step involves evaluation (assessments), education (styles presentation), and explanation (scores of the assessment) of the congregation, individually and corporately. Depending on what will garner the most responses and what works best for a congregation, the assessment can be done any time the church gathers (in Sunday school, at worship, at weekday events) or through the mail. The accuracy of the congregation's overall composition of personalities increases with the number of assessments completed. The results of the assessment are then plotted, outcomes shared with the leadership, and decisions made about training, based on the number of responses under each column. A sample plot chart of one congregation's results is in Chapter 9, with names changed for the sake of anonymity. Education about the styles consists of extensive teaching on the six biblical styles, with a couple of styles divided into substyles. These teaching times focus on the personality-based experiences of various Bible characters as well as on the experiences of Jesus' life.

Step 5: Personality Styles: Specific Training

Notice that the training comes AFTER we know the composition of the congregation as a whole and as individuals. Don't impose any evangelism program on the whole; allow the way God has brought the whole congregation together to indicate how many styles you train your folks in. Some congregations have done simultaneous trainings in all six styles. Smaller churches have found it works better to conduct two trainings of three to four hours each in just two styles, because the largest numbers of congregants show primary and secondary strengths in those dominant styles. This equipping can be done in a classroom setting over several weeks or at a special event during a weekend. It is best to reinforce the in-class training with some hands-on experience, preferably on the same day or weekend of the training. And remember, as the Lord does add people to the congregation, these assessments and training become an ongoing part of the church's discipleship work.

Step 6: Personality Styles: Organic Outreach

This step is more a result than a step. It will come naturally as people discover their styles and then are put together with either like-styled congregants (a homogenous team) or mixed-styled congregants (an eclectic team). These teams are then allowed to dream God's dream to fulfill God's vision for the church. For the training portion, the leadership should come up with experiential learning for each specific style. The people should then be allowed to come up with their own outreach ministry, either as a small group or on behalf of the whole church. There is no need to get people to buy in, because the participants have already been empowered to birth their own outreach. Obviously, the actual outreach and what a group is capable of doing depend upon the church size—or on the group size in a larger church—an on those who are committed to participating.

Step 7: Follow-up and Discipleship

You will need to put in place the means to accommodate newcomers to the church and new believers to Christ. A seeker class on Sundays is one good place to start. A new small group Bible study, preferably home-based, is another idea. What you need in this step is the means to incorporate the new folks who have come into the life of the congregation. This stage provides new people with both a sense of belonging as well as opportunities for responding and believing.

While it might be preferable for congregations to start at Step 1 and move systematically through to Step 7, I recognize that each situation is different. Some of you may use this book as individuals in the beginning. Others of you may be working on it together in groups. Whichever way you get started, rejoice in the beginning and look forward to what the Lord will do in and through you to offer Christ to those in your places of influence.

recommended resources

Disclaimer: This appendix is the result of personally perusing and assessing more than one thousand resources, most of which speak to the theory or general practice of evangelism, but are not style specific, as organized below. This listing is broken down by styles based on my own reading and recommendations by others, as well as online reviews. These resources are across the spectrum of both styles and theological thinking. A given author may not realize that his or her resources are style specific because he or she writes out of his or her natural style. Some resources actually have more than one style, but the dominant style is used in order to place the resource. As with any recommendation, glean the best...disregard the rest. Just because a resource is listed here does not mean that I agree with the complete contents of each item referenced. Resources are not listed in order of preference or priority.

Inclusive of All Six Personality Styles
Nicky Gumbel. *The Alpha Course.* Colorado Springs: Cook Communications, 1993. *The Alpha Course* is the only evangelism methodology that is endorsed by the Office of Evangelism of National Ministries of the American Baptist Churches for use in our nearly six thousand local congregations. It is the only resource inclusive of all six styles of evangelism presented in my book. It is also multigenerational and provides curricula for youth, college-age people, and adults. (There was even, at one time, a children's component called *Alpha Bits.*) The course is a ten-week series of

fifteen sessions introducing seekers to the Christian faith and then challenging participants about halfway through the program to make a faith commitment to Jesus Christ. It was birthed within a charismatic experience and sacramental tradition.

Within *The Alpha Course*, incarnational people are great for setting up, tearing down, and providing the weekly meal. Invitational people are the ones who get new folks to attend. Relational people are the ones who come to the weekly sessions and attend the one-weekend retreat to connect with participants, giving seekers a sense of belonging before believing. The storytelling people are those who share where they have come from and what God has done and continues to do in their lives during the weekly testimony time. The analytical people are those who facilitate the small group discussions as well as actually teach the courses, if the group decides not to go with the recorded messages. The assertive people are the ones who serve best at the weekend retreat, challenging people to act on what they have heard for the past five weeks.

Assertive

Public:
Allison, Lon and Mark Anderson. *Going Public with the Gospel.* Downers Grove, IL: InterVarsity Press, 2004.

Cahill, Mark. *One Thing You Can't Do In Heaven.* Dallas, TX: Biblical Discipleship Ministries, 2002. (Also available in Spanish.)

Carswell, Roger, et al. *Growing Your Church through Discovering and Developing Evangelists.* Fearn, Scotland, UK: Christian Focus Publications, 2000.

Lee, Witness. *Rising Up to Preach the Gospel.* Anaheim, CA: Living Stream Ministry, 2003.

Palau, Luis. *Telling the Story: Evangelism for the Next Generation.* Ventura, CA: Regal Publications, 2006. (Also available in Spanish.)

Personal:

Batzing, Peter and David LeFlore, Jr. *Fast Food Evangelism.* Alachua, FL: Bridge-Logos Publishers, 2007.

Bradley, Carlton. *Soul Winning Is an Attitude.* Lima, OH: CSS Publishing Company, 2000.

Bright, Bill. *How to Introduce Others to Christ.* Orlando: New Life Publications, 2002.

———. *Five Steps to Sharing Your Faith.* Orlando: New Life Publications, 2002.

Davis, Freddy. *Worldview Witnessing: How to Confidently Share Christ with Anyone.* Otsego, MI: PageFree Publishing, 2007.

Gale, Stanley. *Warfare Witness: Contending with Spiritual Opposition in Everyday Evangelism.* Fearn, Tain, Ross-shire, Scotland, UK: Christian Focus Publications, 2006.

Gibbs, Alfred. *Personal Evangelism.* Dubuque, IA: ECS Ministries, 2004.

Smith, Wendell. *From Zero to Eeternity in 60 Seconds Flat: Influencing Others for Christ at a Moment's Notice.* Lake Mary, FL: Charisma House, 2004.

Stebbins, Thomas H. *D. James Kennedy's Explosion of Evangelism.* Fort Lauderdale, FL: Evangelism Explosion Publications, 2002.

Stanley, Andy. *Am I Good Enough? Preparing for Life's Final Exam.* Portland, OR: Multnomah Press, 2005. (Also available in Spanish.)

Training programs and curriculums:

Comfort, Ray. *The School of Biblical Evangelism.* Alachua, FL: Bridge Logos Publishers, 2004. (This book has an accompanying DVD.) (Beltflower, CA: Living Waters Ministries). www.way-ofthemaster.com, accessed May 22, 2009.

Dare To Be A Daniel. Charlotte, NC: Billy Graham Evangelistic Association, 2006. (for tweens)

Lovett, C.S. and Frank W. Moseley. *SOS: How to Be A Successful Soul Winner.* Roeland, KS: SomeOne Special, Inc., 2000. www.soshelp.com, accessed May 22, 2009.

Toler, Stan. *ABCs of Evangelism.* Kansas City, MO: Beacon Hill Press, 2002.

Phenomena:
Addison, Doug. *Prophecy, Dreams, and Evangelism.* North Sutton, NH: Streams Publishing House, 2006. (With study guide)

Ahn, Ché. *Fire Evangelism.* Grand Rapids: Chosen Books, 2006.

———. *Spirit-Led Evangelism: Reaching the Lost through Love and Power.* Grand Rapids: Chosen Books, 2008.

Blasi, Jean Krisle. *Prophetic Fishing: Evangelism in the Power of the Spirit.* Grand Rapids: Chosen Books, 2008.

Maldondo, Guillermo. *Evangelismo Sobrenatural.* Miami, FL: El Rey/ERJ Publications, 2007.

Smith, Sean. *Prophetic Evangelism: Empowering a Generation to Seize Their Day.* Shippensburg, PA: Destiny Image Publishers, 2005.

Analytical

Bickel, Bruce and Stan Jantz. *Why Jesus Matters.* Uhrichsville, OH: Barbour Publishing, 2003.

Bierle, Don. *Surprised By Faith.* McLean, VA: Global Publishing Services, 2003.

Blanch, Jack. *What If God Does Exist?* Enumclaw, WA: Pleasant Word/Winepress Group, 2005.

———. *¿Y si Dios Existe?* Grand Rapids: Editorial Portavoz, 2006.

Boyd, Gregory and Edward Boyd. *Letters from a Skeptic: A Son Wrestles with His Father's Questions about Christianity.* Colorado Springs: David C. Cook Publishing, 2008.

———. *Cartas de un Esceptico.* Miami, FL: Vida, 2004.

Colson, Charles and Harold Fickett. *The Faith*. Grand Rapids: Zondervan, 2008.

D'Souza, Dinesh. *What's so Great about Christianity?* Wheaton, IL: Tyndale House Publishers, 2008.

Geisler, Norman and Patrick Zukeran. *The Apologetics of Jesus: A Caring Approach to Dealing with Doubters*. Grand Rapids: Baker Books, 2009.

Greenleaf, Simon. *The Testimony of the Evangelists Examined by the Rules of Evidence Administrated in Courts of Justice*. Ann Arbor, MI: University of Michigan Library Press, 2006. (The original was published in 1846.)

Ham, Ken. *Why Won't They Listen? A Radical New Approach to Evangelism*. Green Forest, AR: Master Books/New Leaf Press, 2002.

———. *Evangelismo para el Nuevo Milenio*. Green Forest, AR: Master Books/New Leaf Press, 2003.

Harber, Frank. *Sherlock's Faith: The Investigation of Christianity*. Keller, TX: HeartSpring Media, 2004.

Keller, Timothy. *Reason for God: Belief in an Age of Skepticism*. New York: Dutton Adult/Penguin Group, 2008.

Little, Paul. *Know Why You Believe*. Downers Grove, IL: InterVarsity Press, 2008.

Loscalzo, Craig A. *Apologetic Preaching: Proclaiming Christ to a Postmodern World*. Downers Grove, IL: InterVarsity Press, 2000.

McDowell, Josh. *Evidence for Christianity*. Nashville: Thomas Nelson Publishers, 2006.

McDowell, Sean. *Apologetics for a New Generation: A Biblical and Culturally Relevant Approach to Talking about God*. Eugene, OR: Harvest House Publishers, 2009.

McFarland, Alex. *The 10 Most Common Objections to Christianity*. Ventura, CA: Regal Books, 2007.

———. *Las 10 Objeciones Más Comunes Al Cristianismo*. Lake Mary, FL: Casa Creacion, 2008.

Newman, Randy. *Questioning Evangelism*. Grand Rapids: Kregel Publications, 2004.

———. *Evangelice como Jesus*. Grand Rapids: Editorial Portavoz, 2008.

———. *Cornering Conversations: Engaging Dialogues about God and Life*. Grand Rapids: Kregel Publications, 2006.

Orr-Ewing, Amy. *Is Believing in God Irrational?* Downers Grove, IL: InterVarsity Books, 2008.

Pippert, Rebecca. *Hope Has Its Reasons*. Downers Grove, IL: InterVarsity Press, 2001.

Rainer, Thom. *The Unexpected Journey: Conversations with People Who Turned from Other Beliefs to Jesus*. Grand Rapids: Zondervan, 2005.

———. *Un Giro Inesperado*. Miami, FL: Vida, 2007.

Robinson, Stephen. *Questioning Your Faith and Living to Tell About It*. Enumclaw, WA: Pleasant Word/WinePress Publishing, 2004.

Sproul, R.C. *Defending Your Faith: An Introduction to Apologetics*. Wheaton, IL: Crossway Books, 2003.

Strobel, Lee. *The Case for a Creator*. Grand Rapids: Zondervan, 2005.

———. *El Case del Creador*. Miami: Vida, 2005.

———. *Case for Faith*. Grand Rapids: Zondervan, 2000.

———. *El Caso de la Fe*. Miami: Vida, 2001.

Zacharias, Ravi. *Beyond Opinion*. Nashville: Thomas Nelson Publishers, 2008.

———. *Can Man Live without God*. Nashville: Thomas Nelson Publishers, 2004.

———. *The End of Reason*. Grand Rapids: Zondervan, 2008.

Training programs/curriculums:
Zacharias, Ravi. *Jesus Among Other Gods* (Nashville: Thomas Nelson Publishers, 2001). Also available in a curriculum by the same title (Nashville: Thomas Nelson Publishers, 2002).

Hemphill, Ken and Frank Harber. *Got Life?* Keller, TX: Heart-Spring Media, 2000. (Teen-oriented) www.gotlife.org

Meadows, Peter and Joseph Steinberg. *The Y Course.* Bletchley, England, UK: Word Publishing, 1999 (book); 2001 (curriculum).

Tice, Rico. *Christianity Explored.* London, England, UK: All Souls Church/Authentic Media, 2004. www.christianity explored.org

Storytelling

Covell, Jim, Karen Covell, and Victorya Rogers. *How to Talk about Jesus without Freaking Out.* Colorado Springs: Multnomah Books, 2001.

Kallenberg, Brad. *Live to Tell: Evangelism for a Postmodern Age.* Grand Rapids: Brazos Press, 2002.

Metzger, Will. *Tell the Truth: The Whole Gospel to the Whole Person by Whole People.* Downers Grove, IL: InterVarsity Press, 2002.

Moore, R. York. *Growing Your Faith by Giving It Away: Telling the Gospel Story with Grace and Passion.* Downers Grove, IL: InterVarsity Press, 2005.

Moreland, J.P. and Tim Muehlhoff. *The God Conversation: Using Stories and Illustrations to Explain Your Faith.* Downers Grove, IL: InterVarsity Press, 2007.

Newman, Randy. *Questioning Evangelism: Engaging People's Hearts the Way Jesus Did.* Grand Rapids: Kregel Publications, 2004. (with CD of podcasts)

Salter McNeil, Brenda. *A Credible Witness.* Downers Grove, IL: InterVarsity Press, 2008.

Siewert, Alison. *Drama Team Sketchbook: 12 Scripts that Bring the Gospels to Life.* Downers Grove, IL: InterVarsity Press, 2004.

———. *Drama Team Handbook.* Downers Grove, IL: InterVarsity Press, 2003.

Simpson, Michael. *Permission Evangelism.* Colorado Springs: David C. Cook Publisher, 2003.

Stallings, James. *Telling the Story: Evangelism in Black Churches.* Valley Forge, PA: Judson Press, 1988.

Winner, Lauren F. *Girl Meets God.* New York: Random House, 2003.

Training Programs and Curriculums:

Reid, Alvin. *The Net: Evangelism for the 21st Century.* Alpharetta, GA: North American Mission Board, 2000.

3Story. Englewood, CO: Youth for Christ/USA, 2000 (book); 2006 (study guide). (A testimonial-based curriculum geared to teens that focuses on three narrative dramas: God's, their own, and a friend's, who they are trying to reach.)

Relational

Aldrich, Joseph. *Lifestyle Evangelism.* Portland, OR: Multnomah Books, 2006.

Arn, Charles. *White Unto Harvest: Evangelizing Today's Senior Adults.* Monrovia, CA: Institute for American Church Growth, 2003. (This book is a result of a study funded in part by the National Ministries Office of Evangelism in 2000.)

Bettis, Chap. *Evangelism for the Tongue-Tied.* Enumclaw, WA: Pleasant Word/Winepress Group, 2004.

Bulloch, John. *How to Lead Your Loved Ones to the Lord: Six Practical Steps.* Tulsa, OK: Harrison House, 2000.

Burroughs, Esther. *Splash the Living Water: Sharing Jesus in Everyday Moments.* Birmingham, AL: New Hope Publishers, 2006.

Cole, Neil. *Organic Church*. Hoboken, NJ: Jossey-Bass, 2005.

Coleman, Robert. *The Master Plan of Evangelism*. Grand Rapids: Revell, 2006.

Crandall, Ronald. *Witness: Learning to Share your Christian Faith*. Nashville: Discipleship Resources, 2007. (This 25-week small-group study integrates biblical and theological reflection, the practice of spiritual disciplines, and witnessing in the name of Jesus. Workbooks/journals are available.)

Dever, Mark. *The Gospel and Personal Evangelism*. Wheaton, IL: Crossway Books, 2007.

Dreisbach, Bruce. *The Jesus Plan*. Colorado Springs: WaterBrook Press, 2002.

Eastman, Brett and Dee Eastman. *Sharing Christ Together*. Grand Rapids: Zondervan, 2005. (With DVD curriculum)

Geisler, Norman and David Geisler. *Conversational Evangelism: How to Listen and Speak so You Can Be Heard*. Eugene, OR: Harvest House Publishers, 2009.

Henderson, Jim. *Evangelism without Additives: What if Sharing Jesus Meant Just Being Yourself?* Colorado Springs: WaterBrook Press, 2007.

Humphreys, Kent and Davidene Humphreys. *Show and Tell: Presenting the Gospel through Daily Encounters*. Chicago: Moody Publishers, 2000.

Hunter, George. *The Celtic Way of Evangelism*. Nashville: Abingdon Press, 2000.

Langteaux, James Alexander. *God.net: The Journey beyond Belief*. Portland, OR: Multnomah Books, 2001.

McClaren, Brian. *More Ready Than You Realize: Evangelism as Dance in the Postmodern Matrix*. Grand Rapids: Zondervan, 2002.

McIntosh, Duncan. *The Everyday Evangelist*. Valley Forge, PA: Judson Press, 1984

McKee, Jonathan. *Do They Run When They See You Coming?* Grand Rapids: Zondervan/Youth Specialties, 2005. (teen oriented)

McRaney, Will. *The Art of Personal Evangelism: Sharing Jesus in A Changing Culture.* Nashville: Broadman & Holman, 2003.

Morgan, Elisa. *"I Can" Evangelism.* Grand Rapids: Revell, 2008.

———. *Twinkle: Sharing Your Faith One Light at a Time.* Grand Rapids: Revell, 2006.

Peel, William and Walt Larimore. *Going Public with Your Faith: Becoming a Spiritual Influence at Work.* Grand Rapids: Zondervan, 2003.

Peterson, Jim and Mike Shamy. *The Insider.* Colorado Springs: NavPress, 2003.

Pippert, Rebecca. *Out of the Salt Shaker & Into the World.* Downers Grove, IL: InterVarsity Press, 1979.

Prime, Derek. *Active Evangelism.* Ross-Shire, Scotland, UK: Christian Focus Publications, 2003.

Rainer, Thom. *The Unchurched Next Door.* Grand Rapids: Zondervan 2008.

Richardson, Rick. *Evangelism Outside the Box: New Ways to Help People Experience the Good News.* Downers Grove, IL: InterVarsity Press, 2000.

Sorenson, Stephen. *Like Your Neighbor? Doing Everyday Evangelism on Common Ground.* Downers Grove, IL: InterVarsity Press, 2005.

Stebbins, Tom. *Friendship Evangelism by the Book.* Camp Hill, PA: Christian Publications, 1995.

Strobel, Lee. *Como Piensan: Los Incrédulos que Tanto Quiero.* Miami: Vida, 2006.

Tuck, William Powell. *Authentic Evangelism.* Valley Forge, PA: Judson Press, 2002.

Turner, William. *Anytime, Anywhere: Sharing Faith Jesus Style.* Valley Forge, PA: Judson Press, 1997.

Wilkins, Scott. *Reach: A Team Approach To Evangelism and Assimilation.* Grand Rapids: Baker Books, 2005

Training Programs and Curriculums:

Bierle, Don. *Friend to Friend*. Chaska, MN: Faith Studies International, 2001. www.faithsearch.org

Green, Steve and Marijean. *Facing Forever.* Wake Forest, NC: Church Initiative, 2001. www.facingforever.org

Hybels, Bill with Ashley Wiersma. *Just Walk Across the Room: Simple Steps Pointing People to Faith*. Grand Rapids: Zondervan Publishing, 2006.

Lucado, Max. *The 3:16 Promise*. Nashville: Thomas Nelson Publishers, 2007. (with DVD)

————. *3:16: Evangelio de Juan*. Nashville: Thomas Nelson Publishers, 2008.

Mittelberg, Mark and Bill Hybels. *Becoming a Contagious Christian*. Grand Rapids: Zondervan, 1996 (1st ed.); 2007 (2nd ed.). (Comes in adult and youth editions.)

Peel, William and Walt Larimore. *Going Public with Your Faith: Becoming a Spiritual Influence at Work*. Grand Rapids: Zondervan, 2003.

Petersen, Jim and Paul Lutz. *Making Christ Know: Outreach to God*. Chicago: Evangelical Lutheran Church of America, 2001.

Richardson, Rick. *Reimagining Evangelism: Inviting Friends on a Spiritual Journey.* Downers Grove, IL: InterVarsity Press, 2006. (with DVD based curriculum)

Smith, Wallace R. *Baptism Ahead: A Road Map for Young Disciples*. Valley Forge, PA: Judson Press, 2009.

Stanley, Andy. *Go Fish*. Portland: Multnomah Books, 2005 (book); 2007(studyguide/DVD).

Toler, Stan and Louie Bustle. *Each One, Reach One*. Kansas City, MO: Beacon Hill Press, 2007. (with DVD)

Torres, Enrique, Evangelina Snell, and Waldemar Garcia. *Homecoming: A Handbook of Christian Recovery and Evangelism*. Valley Forge, PA: Board of National Ministries ABCUSA, 1999.

Wood, Christine. *Character Witness: How Our Lives Can Make a Difference in Evangelism*. Downers Grove, IL: InterVarsity Press, 2003.

Invitational

Cleave, Derek. *Open Heart, Open Home: A Practical Guide to Evangelism in the Home.* Greenville, SC: Day One Publications, 2000.

Hughes, Page. *Party with a Purpose: Creative Ways to Share Christ.* Birmingham: New Hope Publishers, 2003.

Lefever, Marlene. *Parties with Purpose: Laying the Groundwork for Discipleship and Evangelism.* Colorado Springs: David C. Cook Publications, 2002. (singles ministry resource)

Widening the Circle: Designing Worship that Reaches. Minneapolis: Augsburg Fortress Publishers, 2001.

Wretlind, Norm and Becky Wretlind. *When God Is the Life of the Party.* Colorado Springs: NavPress, 2003.

Training Programs/Events and Curriculums:
Craig, Floyd. *Inviting New Neighbors.* Valley Forge, PA: American Baptist Churches-USA, 1991.

Easter Emphasis (home-based):
Lucado, Max. *He Did This for You.* Nashville: Thomas Nelson Publishers, 2001. (coupled with the book, *He Chose the Nails*)

Lucado, Max. *Lo Hizo por Tí.* Nashville: Thomas Nelson Publishers, 2002.

Invite-A-Friend Kit Options, Any Time of the Year (church-based):
Hershey, S. Joan. *Invite a Friend Kit by New Life Ministries: Sharing Hospitality with New People.* Fort Wayne, IN: LifeQuest, 2004. www.newlifeministries-nlm.org

Bring-A-Friend Sunday (The United Methodist Church) http://www.ntcumc.org/BAFS/index.html 800-969-8201

West Virginia Baptist Convention (ABC). *Reaping Sunday.* Contact director of evangelism and new church planting, Dr. Jack Eades at 304-872-1204 or at eades@wvbc.org

Towns, Elmer and Bill Bryan. *F.R.A.N.tastic Days*. Forest, VA: Church Growth Institute, 1985. Available online for free: http://www.elmertowns.com/books/resourcePkts/FRANtastic/FrantasticDays[ETOWNS].pdf

Incarnational

Briner, Robert. *Roaring Lambs*. Grand Rapids: Zondervan, 2000. (teen oriented)

Ellsworth, Tom. *Beyond Your Backyard: Stepping Out to Serve Others*. Cincinnati: Standard Publishing Company, 2008.

Field Guide to Neighborhood Outreach. Loveland, CO: Group Publishing, 2007.

Johnson, Ron. *From the Outside in: Connecting to the Community Around You*. Atlanta: Lake Hickory Resources, 2006.

Lewis, Robert and Rob Wilkins. *The Church of Irresistible Influence: Bridge-Building Stories to Help Reach Your Community*. Grand Rapids: Zondervan, 2001.

Outreach Ministry in the 21st Century. Loveland, CO: Group Publishing, 2007.

Paris, Jenell Williams and Margot Eyring. *Urban Disciples: A Beginners Guide to Serving God in the City*. Valley Forge, PA: Judson Press, 2000.

Pate, Stephen. *Evangelism Where You Live*. Atlanta: Chalice Press, 2008.

Pierson, Robert D. *Needs-Based Evangelism: Becoming a Good Samaritan Church*. Nashville: Abingdon Press, 2006.

Pilavachi, Mike and Liza Hoeksma. *When Necessary Use Words: Changing Lives through Worship, Justice, and Evangelism*. Ventura, CA: Regal Books, 2007.

Rizzo, Dino. *Servolution: Starting a Church Revolution through Serving*. Grand Rapids: Zondervan, 2009.

Rusaw, Rick and Eric Swanson. *The Externally Focused Church*.

Loveland, CO: Group Publishing, 2004.

Sider, Ron. *Doing Evangelism Jesus' Way: How Christians Demonstrate the Good News.* Nappanee, IN: Evangel Publishing House, 2003.

Sider, Ronald, Philip Olson, and Heidi Rolland Unruh. *Churches that Make a Difference: Reaching Your Community with Good News and Good Works.* Grand Rapids: Baker Books, 2002.

Sjogren, Steve. *Conspiracy of Kindness.* Ventura, CA: Regal Publications, 2008.

————. *101 Ways to Reach Your Community.* Colorado Springs: NavPress Publishing Group, 2000.

Sjogren, Steve and David Ping. *Outflow.* Loveland, CO: Group Publishing, 2007.

Sjogren, Steve, Dave Ping, and Doug Pollock. *Irresistible Evangelism.* Loveland, CO: Group Publishing, 2003.

Sjogren, Steve and Janie Sjogren. *101 Ways to Help People in Need.* Colorado Springs: NavPress Publishing Group, 2002.

They Will Know Us by Our Love: Service Ideas for Small Groups. Loveland, CO: Group Publishing, 2007.

Training Programs/Curriculums:

His Heart, Our Hands: Service Evangelism. Alpharetta, GA: North American Mission Board, 2000.

Outflow: Service Evangelism. Loveland, CO: Group Publishing, 2006. (Adult & Youth Versions)

Millard, M. Kent and Lori Crantford. *Go Fish! T.I.M.E. (Together In Ministry Everyday).* Nashville: Abingdon Press, 2009.

Servant Evangelism. Nashville: Abingdon Press, 2009. Servant evangelism.org got style?

Romans Road of Salvation	Evangelism Explosion	Steps to Peace with God	4 Spiritual Laws	
Traditional	D. James Kennedy	Billy Graham	Bill Bright	
Romans 3:23 All have sinned	Eternal Life is a free gift	#1 God's Purpose: Peace and Life	God loves you	
Romans 6:23 Wages of sin is death	Human beings are sinners	#2 The Problem: Our Separation	Human beings are sinful and separated	
Romans 5:8 Christ died for us	God is merciful	#3 God's Bridge: The Cross	Jesus is the only provision	
Romans 10:9-10 Confess and believe	Jesus is the only way	#4 Our Response: Our Response	We must individually receive	
Romans 5:1 Justified by faith, we have peace with God	God is merciful			
	Salvation is by faith			

SCRIPTED PRESENTATIONS UNDER ASSERTIVE STYLES OF THE GOSPEL

Bridge Illustration	SOS: Scriptures on Salvation	7 Share Scriptures	Dare2Share
Dawson Trotman	Frank Moseley	Bill Fay	Greg Stier
We matter to God	State of Sinners Romans 3:23	Romans 3:23 For all have sinned	**G**od created us to be with him
We rebelled against God	Sentence of Sinners Romans 6:23	Romans 6:23 Wages of sin is death	**O**ur sins separate us from God
Jesus is the only answer	Source of Salvation John 3:16	John 3:3 Must be born again	**S**ins cannot be removed by good deed
We must believe, repent, and receive	Shortcoming of Service Titus 3:5	John 14:6 Jesus is the only way	**P**aying the price for sin, Jesus died
	Simplicity of Salvation Revelation 3:20	Romans 10:9-10 You must confess	**E**veryone who trusts in Jesus alone has eternal life
	Securing our Salvation Sinner's Prayer	2 Corinthians 5:15 No longer live for self	**L**ife that's eternal means we will live with Jesus forever
		Revelation 3:20 Answer the door	

Primary Style	Assertive			Analytical	Storytelling	Relational	Invitational	Incarnational
	a. Proclamation	b. Personal	c. 1. Prophetic 2. Power					
Training Programs and Resources	(1) Evangelist Preaching Course (Billy Graham Ctr)	(1) Evangelism Explosion (Kennedy)	(1) Surprised by the Power of the Holy Spirit	(1) Got Life? (teen-oriented)	The Net	(1) The Alpha Course	Invite a Friend:	a. Service—short term
	(2) Telephone Usage	(2) Share Jesus without Fear (Fay)	(2) How to have a Healing Ministry in any Church	(2) Jesus among many gods		(2) The Everyday Commandment (CPR)	a. Home-based Love Thy Neighbor(hood)	(1) Servant Evangelism (Cincinnati Vineyard)
	a. Real Call proactive	(3) Witnessing without Fear (Bright)	(3) Association of Healing Rooms	(3) The 'Y' Course		(3) Facing Forever	b. Church-based He did this for you	(2) ABC Aid Center www.sturgi-said.com (FBC, Deadwood, SD)
	b. GoTel reactive	(4) S.O.S. (Mosley)	(4) www.propheticevangelism.com			(4) Living Proof Evangelism (Peterson)	– Easter Focused Honor Our	b. Servant—long term
	(3) Tract Distribution	(5) ABC Plan (Davis)				(5) People Sharing Jesus	– anytime of the year	(1) Meeting needs "Sharing Christ
	(4) Direct Mailing (Outreach Marketing)	(6) Smart Fishing (McClung)				(6) Live the Life (teen)	– Inviting Neighbors (NM Staff~1990's)	(2) His Heart "Our Hands
		(7) Dare2Share (teen)				(7) Lifestyle Evangelism (teen)		
						(8) Peer-to-Peer (teen)		
						(9) H2O (postmodern)		

Liked *Got Style?* Check out these other Judson Press evangelism books!

Authentic Evangelism:
Sharing the Good News with Sense and Sensitivity
William Powell Tuck

"It's more than a thoroughly practical manual in evangelism; it's a thoughtful review of the biblical and theological bases for effectively 'Sharing the Good News.' The book is a good read, interestingly written, and clearly penned by one who believes in evangelism and has practiced it effectively. It's spiced with the author's personal experiences on the journey, and is richly illustrated...A splendid work, desperately needed." —*Sharing the Practice*: The International Quarterly Journal of the Academy of Parish Clergy   978-0-8170-1415-5, $15.00

Evangelism on Purpose: A Planning Guide for Churches
Richard E. Rusbuldt

This concise and practical guide shows pastors and church leaders how to listen to God's will and expectations for their congregation and open the door to a vital new future as an evangelizing community. Includes questions for discussion at the end of each chapter, along with a leader's guide and workshop outlines.
978-0-8170-0894-9, $7.00

Anytime, Anywhere:
Sharing Faith Jesus Style
William L. Turner

Discover how Jesus shared his faith with those he encountered and learn how to share your faith "Jesus style."
978-0-8170-1260-1, $10.00

The Everyday Evangelist
Duncan McIntosh

This short volume offers simple ways to be an "everyday evangelist" and share the Good News of Jesus Christ with those around you—neighbors, friends, and acquaintances. Excellent group study includes leader helps.   978-0-8170-1042-3, $5.00

To order, call 800-458-3766,
or visit www.judsonpress.com

Save 20% when you

JUDSON PRESS
PUBLISHERS SINCE 1824